# Mastering Harbour Street

*A Guide to Investing in the Jamaica Stock Exchange*

## by O'neil Francis

Production and Layout:
Guyenterprise


ISBN 978-976-96173-1-5

*To my father, Rupert Francis, the most generous man I know; and to my mother, Wildia Francis, the personification of prudent financial management.*

# Acknowledgements

I could not have written this book without the encouragement and assistance of a large number of persons, to all of whom I express gratitude. I would also like to thank, in particular, Ms. Marlene Street Forrest, Managing Director of the Jamaica Stock Exchange, who graciously agreed to meet with me during the preparation of the manuscript. Our general discussion on the successes of the stock exchange was very instructive and inspired me to make extremely useful improvements to the text. I, of course, take full responsibility for any errors or omissions.

Finally, I would like to express my deep gratitude to my sister, Dr. Patrice Francis-Emmanuel, and to Melanie Gilchrist and Alicia Reid for their encouragement.

# Contents

## CHAPTER THREE

# The Essential Commandments
# of Stock Investing

CHAPTER ONE

# THE JAMAICA STOCK EXCHANGE

Why Invest in Stocks?

The History of the Jamaica Stock Exchange

The Role and Objectives of the Jamaica Stock Exchange

The JSE as a Source of Wealth Creation

The JSE: The World's Best Performing Stock Market

Stocks vs Treasury Bills, Bonds and Other Assest Classes in Jamaica

Future Sources of Growth of the JSE

The Current Structure of the JSE

# THE JAMAICA STOCK EXCHANGE

## Why Invest in Stocks?

The Jamaica Stock Exchange ("JSE"), located on Harbour Street, has captured the imagination of the financial world. With the success of the Jamaica Stock Exchange, Harbour Street is rapidly becoming the new epicentre of wealth creation in Jamaica. The aim of this book is to demonstrate, as clearly as possible, how to master the game of stock investing and how Harbour Street may hold the key to your financial freedom. My hope is that with the help of this book you will learn what it takes to master the game.

A paycheck is almost never sufficient to make a decent living. A 9:00 - 5:00 job often rarely pays at a level which makes most individuals financially secure. Most of us must therefore invest in order to be able to accumulate enough to live comfortably. I will take care to show you how disciplined investors who use the tools available for successful investing can leverage the stock market to help them in the process of accumulating enough to become financially secure.

The stock market has traditionally been one of the best sources for wealth creation. Many studies done across the world consistently show that stocks almost always outperform other asset classes such as real estate, bonds and treasury bills. The results of these studies in other markets also apply to the Jamaican market. This is because, as in other markets, companies grow over time and reward investors accordingly. Other asset classes tend to grow at a much slower pace over time and generally underperform stocks in all instances.

Let us look at the United States market as an example. In 1964, Professors James H. Lorie and Lawrence Fisher of the University of Chicago confirmed that stocks offered significantly higher returns even through the stock market crash of 1929, the Great Depression and World War II[1]. According to both professors, stocks returned 9 per cent higher returns per year than any other investment class in the 35 years from 1926 to 1960. The most turbulent developments in world history marked this period. However, neither wars, market crashes nor financial turmoil were enough to overturn the general upward trend of the stock market.

What was true between 1926 and 1960 was also true between 1925 and 2014. Over that 89-year period, stocks outperformed all other asset classes by leaps and bounds in real terms[2]. Therefore, historically, after accounting for inflation, stockholders, over a long period, will normally amass far more real wealth than holders of other assets. Each US$1 invested in U.S. stocks in 1925 was worth US$405 in real inflation adjusted terms in 2014. US$1 invested in long term U.S. treasury bonds was worth US$10.32 over the same period. US$1 invested in treasury bills was worth US$1.57, while US$1 invested in gold was worth US$4.47 in 2014. US$1 left under a mattress in cash was worth 8 cents after 89 years due to the erosion of its value by inflation[3].

Graphically, the picture is telling:

| Investment in 1925 US $ | Real Value in 2014 US $ | per cent gain in 89 years |
|---|---|---|
| $1 invested in **Stocks** | $405 | 40,400% |
| $1 invested in **Long-Term US$ Treasury Bonds** | $10.32 | 932% |
| $1 invested in **Treasury Bills** | $1.57 | 57% |
| $1 invested in **Gold** | $4.47 | 347% |
| $1 left in **Cash** | $0.08 | -92% |

But no-one has the luxury of investing for 89 years. What about a shorter more modest period such as 20 years? A 20-year investment in stocks would no doubt be reasonable for, say, a 45 year old. Let's take the 20 year period of 1995 to 2014.

An investment of US$1.00 invested in U.S. stocks for the 20 years since 1995 would have resulted in a total of US$4.17 after accounting for inflation at the end of 2014[4]. An investment of US$1 in US Government bonds in 1995 would be worth US$3.33 in 2014. The story of treasury bills is disheartening: US$1 after 20 years would be worth a mere US$1.08 in 2014. By contrast, US$1.00 in Gold at the end of 1995 would be worth US$2.00 at the end of 2014. US$1 in cash in 1995 was only worth US$0.64[5].

The following graph illustrates the point:

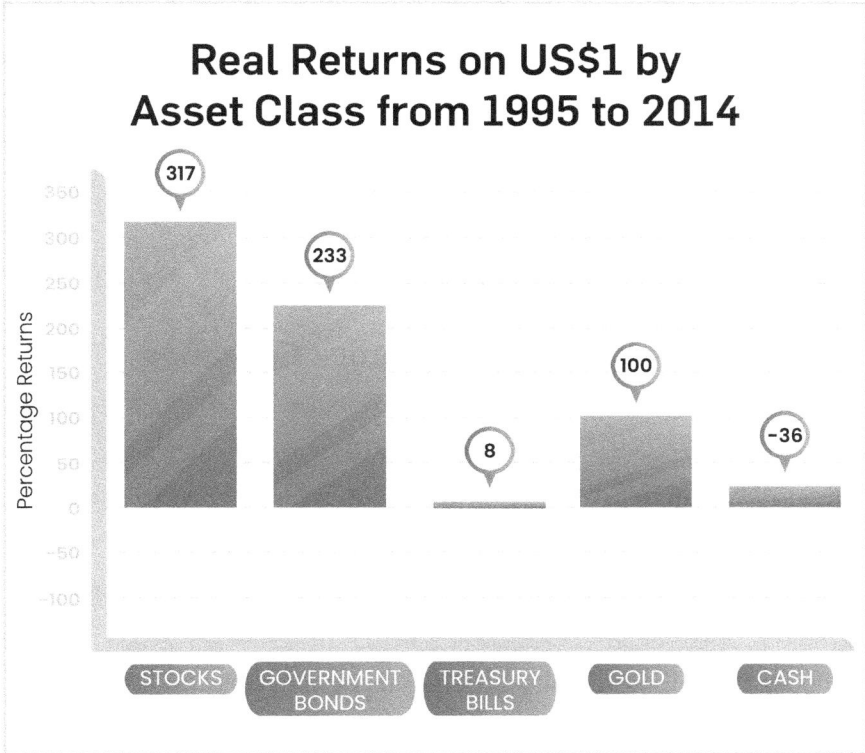

## Real Returns on US$1 by Asset Class from 1995 to 2014

(Percentage Returns)

- STOCKS: 317
- GOVERNMENT BONDS: 233
- TREASURY BILLS: 8
- GOLD: 100
- CASH: -36

Peter Lynch, a respected investment adviser and former head of Fidelity Magellan Fund, a successful U.S. mutual fund, is also absolute in his conviction that stock investments over the long run are far superior to investments in other asset classes. Based on Lynch's research, since 1927, stocks returned an average 9.8 per cent per annum to investors compared to 5 per cent for corporate bonds and 3.4 per cent for treasury bills[6].

You may argue that the figures relate to the United States market. However, most if not all stock markets perform in the same way when compared to bonds, treasury bills and other asset classes. There is no compelling reason to conclude that in the Jamaican context the opposite would be true. Having looked at the historical performance of the U.S. market as a prototype for other stock markets, let's now look more closely at the Jamaica Stock Exchange which, over time, has also performed in a manner that has returned superior results to other markets such as bond markets.

## The History of the Jamaica Stock Exchange

The Jamaica Stock Exchange was incorporated in 1968 and began its operations at the Bank of Jamaica Building on 3rd February, 1969. The JSE was an important institution in post-independence Jamaica's development. It created a means for local companies to raise capital and expand their operations to serve the newly independent society.

The four founding members of the JSE Group were[7]:

- Mr. Willard Samms – Annett & Company Limited;
- Mr. Raglan I. Golding – Capital Market Services (Ja) Ltd;
- Mr. Edward E. Gayle – Edward Gayle & Company Ltd; and
- Mr. Anthony Lloyd – Pitfield Mckay Ross & Co Ltd.

Since it began its operations in 1969, the JSE has grown exponentially. In June 1969, the JSE listed 34 companies, including Caymanas Park, Desnoes and Geddes, Key Homes, Life of Jamaica, Montego Bay Ice Co, Hardware and Lumber, Jamaica Public Service Co., Jamaica Omnibus Services, Guinness Jamaica, Royal Bank of Jamaica, Dyoll, and Caribbean Cement Company. Some of these companies were either acquired by other companies, renamed or delisted. In the 1980s, companies such as GraceKennedy and Seprod also listed.

In the early days of the JSE, most of the shares of companies were tightly held by the families that owned the companies or by overseas parent companies. Only small amounts of shares in those companies were sold to the general public.

## The Role and Objectives of the Jamaica Stock Exchange

The Jamaica Stock Exchange provides the opportunity for businesses that need capital to grow and expand by approaching the public for funding. It also provides the public with the opportunity to invest in businesses by owning a proportion or a slice of that company.

The Jamaica Stock Exchange lists its functions as providing an additional channel for encouraging and mobilizing domestic savings; fostering the growth of the domestic financial services sector; providing savers with greater opportunities to protect themselves against inflation; increasing the overall efficiency of investment; facilitating privatization; improving the gearing of the domestic corporate sector; and helping to reduce corporate dependence on borrowing.

It also lists its objectives as[8]:

- Promoting the orderly and transparent development of the stock market and the stock exchange in Jamaica;
- Ensuring that the stock market and its broker members operate at the highest standards practicable;
- Developing, applying and enforcing the rules designed to ensure public confidence in the stock market and its broker members;

- Providing facilities for the transaction of stock market business; and
- Conducting research, disseminating relevant information and maintaining local and international relationships that can enhance the development of the Jamaican stock market.

## The JSE as a Source of Wealth Creation

The history of the JSE has shown that over the long run stocks are a very good method of building wealth. While the market has had both bad and good years, over a long period, the general trend has been that the market has moved upward. The history of the exchange shows therefore that investors who buy stocks in well-managed, stable companies and hold them over the long term have done well in the past. There is reason to expect that this trend will continue over time as companies grow their businesses. This is the general trend in most stock markets globally, including in Jamaica. An investor who wants to build wealth should therefore consider the JSE as a good option.

The JSE index gives a general picture of how the growth of companies over time has created value for investors. As a hypothetical example, if an investor was able to invest in all the companies in the exchange, that is, if his investment was able to track the index as it went up and down over the years, he would have been very successful by simply holding those stocks over the long run. You could consider the value of the index over time as a proxy of how his wealth would have accumulated. Between June 1969 and February 10, 1978, the index moved from 100 to 35.84[9]. An investor who invested in all the stocks on the market would therefore have seen his wealth decline in tandem with the index. This was the general trend in the 1970s as the market moved downwards, but investors who were patient would have reaped great rewards from March 1978 onwards when the trend was generally upwards. From a low of 35.84 in March 1978, the market moved up to a high of 2,592 points in December 1989, and thereby increased the wealth of investors who kept invested in the market over the long term. By the end of 1991, the index had reached another high of 7,681.50[10].

The JSE also compares favourably with other major stock markets as a source of building real wealth. In an early, and admittedly now dated, study Richard Kitchen noted that over the period 1969-1985, for example, the real annual rate of return on the Jamaica Stock Exchange adjusted for the devaluation of the Jamaican dollar was 10.5% in US$ terms and 7.5% in Pound Sterling terms[11]. These annual rates of return compared favourably to returns on Wall Street and the London Stock Exchange.  In other words, an investor in Jamaican stocks would have done just as well in Jamaica as he would have done in the U.S. or London, even when the return is measured in US$ instead of Jamaican dollars.

Although that study is dated, the evidence suggests that the same holds true currently, especially with the significant growth in the JSE between 2015 and 2018.

## The JSE: The World's Best Performing Stock Market

The 18 January, 2019 edition of Bloomberg's Businessweek Magazine, one of the most respected business news outlets, ranked the JSE as the best performing stock market in the world in 2018. According to Bloomberg, in 2018, Jamaica's main stock market index rose 29 per cent in U.S. dollar terms. This was the highest increase among 94 exchanges worldwide tracked by Bloomberg, beating the New York Stock Exchange, the London FTSE, the CAC in Paris and all other major developed and emerging market stock exchanges. This was a significant accomplishment for the JSE and demonstrated the potential for massive levels of wealth creation for investors in the Jamaican stock market.

The more important point is the consistency in the market's performance. 2018 was not the only year in which the JSE outperformed. In its story on the JSE, Bloomberg also reported that in the five years ending in 2018, the JSE outperformed other markets.

In that period, Jamaican stocks increased almost 300 per cent, more than four times the next best performing market and seven times the Standard and Poor's 500 (S&P500) benchmark. This statistic easily demonstrates the quality, consistency and potential of Jamaican stocks as superior investment vehicles.

The table below further illustrates the point.

| Index | Approximate 5 Year Performance to 4 January 2019[12] |
|---|---|
| Jamaica Stock Exchange | 300% |
| S & P 500 (USA) | 41.43% |
| Dow Jones Industrial Average (USA) | 47.57% |
| FTSE 100 (UK) | 2.61% |
| DAX (Germany) | 14.65% |
| CAC (Paris) | 13.83% |
| Nikkei 225 (Japan) | 27.10% |
| Hang Seng Index (Hong Kong) | 14.15% |
| CSI 300 Index (Shanghai, China) | 35.19% |

Graphically represented, the performance of these markets is as follows:

**5 Year Performance of Major Stock Markets**

An investor in Jamaican stocks could therefore do much better than investing on Wall Street or in London or Paris or in any of the other stock markets worldwide tracked by Bloomberg.

## Stocks vs Treasury Bills, Bonds and Other Asset Classes in Jamaica

Stocks also performed better than treasury bills and bonds and other forms of investment in Jamaica over the period 2014 to 2018 and are likely to continue to outperform those instruments. Jamaica's improved economic environment from 2013 to 2018 led to lower interest rates on bank deposits and other forms of investment. This augurs well for the stock market if Jamaica's economic recovery continues.

Some examples of how $100,000 invested in selected stocks has performed compared to other asset classes since 2014 are instructive[13].

For example, an investment of $100,000 in Kingston Wharves in 2014 would be worth a total of $1,286,448 at the end of 2018. The same investment in Caribbean Cement would be worth $1,759,303 over the same period while the same investment in treasury bills would only be worth $122,013.

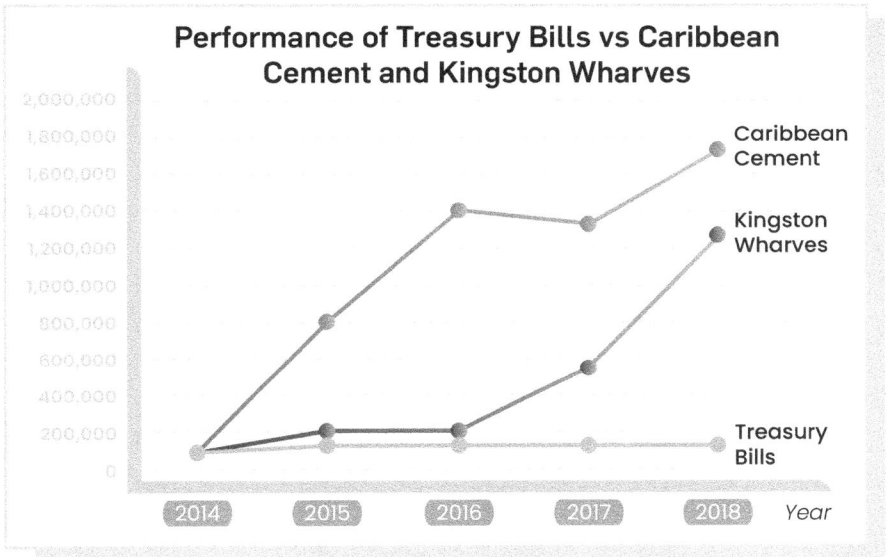

Performance of Treasury Bills vs Caribbean Cement and Kingston Wharves

An investment in those two stocks would therefore have proved far more beneficial than an investment in treasury bills.

Similarly, the value of an investment of $100,000 in Jamaica Broilers in 2014 would be $599,159 at the end of 2018. A similar investment in Berger Paints would be worth $1,291,164 over the same period.

Those results were also far superior to a $100,000 investment in a bond at a hypothetical 5.5% return assuming the principal value remained unchanged and taking account of a 25% tax rate on interest. An investment in bonds would be worth far less than an investment in stocks as the bonds would only be worth $120,051 at the end of 2018.

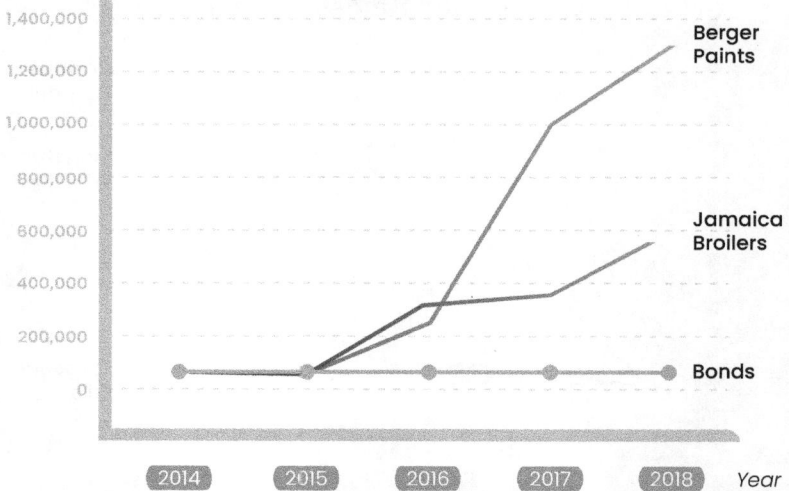

Performance of Bonds vs Jamaica Broilers and Berger Paints

The superiority of stocks is even more pronounced when compared to ordinary savings accounts. An investment of $100,000 in NCB Financial Group would be worth $832,199 at the end of 2018 compared to a total of $105,197 left in a savings account from 2014 to 2018, with a hypothetical rate of 1.5% with interest reinvested after tax.

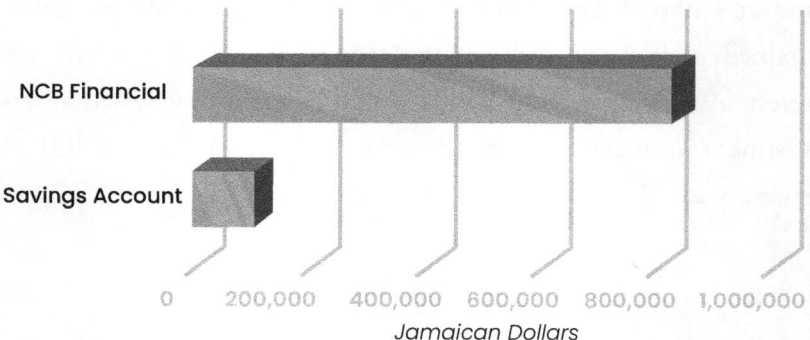

Performance of a Savings Account vs Stocks in NCB Financial Group from 2014 to 2018

The above comparisons are also in tabular form for ease of reference.

| Asset | 2014 | 2015 | 2016 | 2017 | 2018 |
|---|---|---|---|---|---|
| Kingston Wharves 16,666 shares | $100,000 | $189,325 | $196,658 | $541,645 | $1,286,448 |
| Caribbean Cement Company Ltd. | $100,000 | $789,611 | $1,443,956 | $1,346,862 | $1,759,303 |
| Jamaica Broilers Group 20,618 shares | $100,000 | $105,151 | $292,569 | $349,887 | $599,159 |
| Berger Paints 58,823 shares | $100,000 | $94,705 | $228,233 | $973,520 | $1,291,164 |
| NCB Financial Group 5,577 shares | $100,000 | $153,208 | $231,724 | $485,310 | $832,199 |
| Bond[14] | $100,000 | $104,675 | $109,568 | $114,690 | $120,051 |
| Tresury Bills[15] | $100,000 | $105,100 | $110,460 | $116,093 | $122,013 |
| Bank Savings Account[16] | $100,000 | $101,275 | $102,566 | $103,873 | $105,197 |

Based on the above examples, the performance of individual companies and the market in general are therefore good indications of opportunities for investment.

## Future Sources of Growth of the JSE

While the stock exchange has grown in the past, it is important to consider what factors will continue to propel growth in the future. I see three critical factors: namely the diaspora, improving economic fundamentals and growing investor interest.

## The Diaspora

The JSE offers great potential for wealth creation not only for Jamaicans at home but Jamaicans living in the Diaspora as well. Many Jamaicans overseas have access to significant levels of savings and could earn higher returns in Jamaican stocks than they earn in their adopted homes. Interest rates in the United States, Canada and the United Kingdom have been at historic lows since the 2008 global financial crisis, and many asset classes in those countries have yielded inferior returns when compared to the Jamaica Stock Exchange. Members of the Diaspora, hoping to find a good vehicle for wealth creation, should therefore consider the Jamaica Stock Exchange as a good option.

The Diaspora is a potentially significant source of future growth for the JSE; and in turn, the JSE is a key source of wealth creation for the Diaspora. Members of the Diaspora are well aware of this fact. In his statement during a visit to the JSE by delegates of the Jamaica 55 Diaspora Conference held in Kingston in July 2017, Mr. Marlon Hill, a former Jamaican Diaspora Advisory Board Member for the Southern United States, speaking on behalf of the delegates, summarized the important link between the Diaspora and the JSE. As he stated, *"This historic occasion is a testament to our Jamaican diaspora stories worldwide and offers an opportunity for us to make a meaningful contribution to Jamaica's national development and to simultaneously build wealth for our families. We have a choice of where to put our personal wealth, either on Wall Street or Harbour Street."* [17]

It is clear that the objectively high performance of the JSE and the growing interest of the Diaspora will bode well for increased demand for Jamaican stocks and continued growth of the JSE into the future.

## Economic Fundamentals

Many factors influence how well the stock market does and, by extension, how well you will do by investing in stocks. One important factor to bear in mind is that stock markets in stable economies that improve basic economic indicators over time tend to grow as consumers and investors develop confidence in the future. The Jamaican economy has improved in a number of areas since 2015. The total national debt when measured against the country's Gross Domestic Product (GDP) fell significantly. As a result of deliberate Government policy, the national debt also continued to trend downward. If Government borrowing and debt levels continue to fall, more financing will be available for companies to expand and increase earnings thus enhancing their value and ability to pay dividends.

Falling interest rates are also good for the stock market. When interest rates on government short term treasury bills in Jamaica hovered around 20 per cent, an investor could simply place his money in those investment instruments without the need to risk investing in the stock market. But as interest rates fall, it becomes less attractive for investors to invest in treasury bills or bonds or to save in traditional savings accounts. They search for more attractive options. The stock market is often one of the most attractive options and yields the highest returns in a low interest rate environment.

In 2019, interest rates in Jamaica were at single digit levels having fallen from double-digit levels in the 1990s. This development, if sustained over the long term, also bodes well for the future growth of the Jamaican stock market.

### Growing Investor Interest

The Jamaican population has traditionally not invested heavily in stocks. The Jamaica Stock Exchange was established with a relatively small number of companies listed and investment in stocks was concentrated in very few hands. As time progressed, the percentage of the Jamaican population that has invested in stocks has slowly increased. The percentage of the Jamaican population invested in equities moved, over time, from a low of 2 per cent to 15 per cent in 2018. This figure is still low compared to the global average of 25 per cent. The trend, however, has been positive, as Jamaicans have become more aware of the advantages of investing in the stock market. As the market continues to do well and if interest rates continue to fall, more ordinary Jamaicans will become investors in the market. As more investors enter the market and the demand for stocks increases, there should also be more growth and greater returns for investors.

## The Current Structure of the JSE

Both ordinary and preference shares trade on the JSE and ownership of those shares has become less concentrated. Shares of Jamaican companies are therefore much more widely held not only by large institutions such as banks and insurance companies but also by individual investors.

The shares listed on the Exchange fall into several major categories, namely finance and insurance services, manufacturing, trading, communications, transportation, tourism, entertainment, and distribution services. There are discrete markets, namely the Main Market, the Junior Market and the US$ Market. The Jamaica Social Stock Exchange for not-for-profit entities was launched in January 2019 and will evolve over time as the law permits. The new exchange will support entities in solving social, cultural, economic or environmental problems. There are also plans afoot to add other options to the JSE.

The Main Market is the most important market. It allows trade in shares of large, older and more established companies while the Junior Market trades in shares of small and medium sized companies some of which were recently established. The Junior Market encourages entrepreneurship and business development of smaller companies by offering certain tax incentives when they list on that market. Companies that list on the Junior Market receive a full income tax holiday for the first 5 years of the company's life on the Market and a 50 per cent income tax relief for the next 5 years. Each company listed on the Junior Market must have stated capital of not less than J$50 million and not more than J$500 million following its initial public offer.

# Notes

[1]   Rates of Return on Investments in Common Stock "Journal of Business" (January 1964), pp 1-21.

[2]   Stocks, Bonds, Bills and Inflation and Gold: Originally written summer 2001 and updated annually and last updated April 27, 2015 by Shawn Allen, CFA, CMA, MBA, P.Eng. at **http://www.investorsfriend.com/asset-performance/.**
**Last visited 28 March 2016**

[3]   Stocks, Bonds, Bills and Inflation and Gold: Originally written summer 2001 and updated annually and last updated April 27, 2015 by Shawn Allen, CFA, CMA, MBA, P.Eng. at **http://www.investorsfriend.com/asset-performance/.**
**Last visited 28 March 2016**

[4]   Stocks, Bonds, Bills and Inflation and Gold: Originally written summer 2001 and updated annually and last updated April 27, 2015 by Shawn Allen, CFA, CMA, MBA, P.Eng. at **http://www.investorsfriend.com/asset-performance/.**
**Last visited 28 March 2016**

[5]   Stocks, Bonds, Bills and Inflation and Gold: Originally written summer 2001 and updated annually and last updated April 27, 2015 by Shawn Allen, CFA, CMA, MBA, P.Eng. at **http://www.investorsfriend.com/asset-performance/.**
**Last visited 28 March 2016**

[6]   Peter Lynch- One Up on Wall Street p.70

[7]   **https://www.jamstockex.com/about/**

[8]   **https://www.jamstockex.com/about/**

[9]   Terrence D. Agbeyegbe- Some Stylised Facts about the Jamaica Stock Market, Social and Economic Studies  Vol. 43, No 4 (December 1994) , pp 143-156

[10]  Terrence D. Agbeyegbe- Some Stylised Facts about the Jamaica Stock Market, Social and Economic Studies  Vol. 43, No 4 (December 1994) , pp 143-156

[11]  Richard Kitchen- The Role of the Jamica Stock Exchange in the Capital Market: A Historical Analysis, Savings and Development  Vol 11, No. 3 (1987) pp. 249- 274.

[12]  Figures, except for the JSE figure, taken from Bloomberg Markets **https://www.bloomberg.com/markets/stocks. Last visited January 24 2019.** The figure for the JSE was reported in Businessweek's January 18, 2019 edition.

[13]  The growth in the value of stock investments is approximate, based on the closing price for each year as reported in the Jamaica Stock Exchange Yearbook 2017 and the JSE closing price for 2018 on the JSE website. It also excludes dividends. The growth in the value of other asset classes assumes that interest payments are reinvested over the five year period and are compounded after deducting applicable taxes.

[14]  At a hypothetical 5.5% return assuming the principal value remains unchanged and taking account of a 25% tax rate on interest. These are approximate figures.

[15]  At a hypothetical consistent average of 6% return on a 182 day instrument, assuming the principal value plus interest are reinvested immediately on maturity, taking account of a 25% tax rate on interest. These are approximate figures.

[16]  Represents a hypothetical bank savings account rate at 1.5% return with interest reinvested after tax.

[17]  **https://www.jamstockex.com/jses-historic-closing-bell-ceremony-with-members-of-the-jamaican-diaspora/**

# THE BASICS OF STOCK INVESTING

What are Stocks?

Dividends

Price Appreciation

What is a Stock Split

Initial Public Offerings (IPOS)

How to Buy Shares in an IPO

How to Buy and Sell Listed Stocks on the JSE

Services to be Expected of Your Stock Broker

What to Consider When Choosing Your Broker

Practical Considerations When Trading Stocks

When not to Invest in the Stock Market

How to Read the Stock Tables

The Environment that Influences Stocks

Where to Find Information on Listed Companies

The Risks of Investing in Stocks

# THE BASICS OF STOCK INVESTING

## What are Stocks?

Stocks, also called "shares" or "equity", are a type of asset that represents ownership of part of a business or a company. A stockholder is therefore part owner of a company. The proportion of the company that stockholders own is dependent on the number of shares they own as a percentage of the total number of shares the company has issued. Therefore, if a company has issued 1,000,000 shares and one person has bought 10,000 shares, he owns 1% of the company.

There are two main types of shares, namely ordinary and preference shares. Ordinary shares generally entitle the shareholder to the right to vote at company stockholder meetings and to receive dividends. Preference shares entitle the investor to certain rights and privileges over the ordinary shareholder such as receiving payments of dividends before ordinary shareholders do. They however do not normally have voting rights but are entitled to the first right of payment if the company were to go bankrupt.

A share or stock in a company entitles the stockholder to a share in the company's dividends.

## Dividends

Dividends are a company's distribution of a percentage of its after tax profits to its stockholders. The company's board of directors determines whether a dividend should be paid, the amount of dividends paid to shareholders and the frequency of those payments. Some companies pay dividends on an annual basis, while some companies pay biannually or on a quarterly basis depending on what schedule aligns with their internal accounting procedures. In addition to its regularly scheduled dividend, a company may also pay special dividends occasionally to reward shareholders when the company enjoys an especially good year.

For example, in 2015, in addition to a $0.97 dividend, **Seprod** paid an additional special dividend to its shareholders of $2.28, generated from a one-off gain it made from a sale of assets that year[18]. Similarly, in June 2019, **Scotia Group Jamaica Limited** announced a second interim dividend of 0.51 cents and a special dividend of $1.94. The special dividend was paid from accumulated earnings over previous years.

For each share, a company pays a specific dollar value of dividend. This can be measured as a percentage of the value of each stock. For example, if each share is worth $50.00, and a company pays a dividend of $0.50 per share each year, stockholders earn a dividend of 1% of the value of their shares. Without doing anything other than hold the stock, the investor earns a return: that is, he is earning what is called a dividend yield of one per cent per year on his investment simply by holding the stock.

Dividend payouts may vary among companies with some paying larger dividend ratios than others. Dividends typically range from as much as 7% to as little as below 1%. The average yield for stocks in Jamaica is less than 2%. Some well-established companies, as a reward to investors, consistently increase their dividends annually. The longer investors hold those company shares, the more they will earn from dividends. Among the companies that consistently increase dividends are **GraceKennedy Group and Seprod Limited** which in 2016 had increased its dividends annually for 10 years[19].

Investors who wish to build wealth would be well advised to consider investing in dividend paying companies that build their wealth with each dividend payment. The more dividend you would like to be paid, the more of the company's stock you need to own. Over the long run, dividends have proved to be a good way of accumulating wealth.

The longer you hold stocks and receive dividends, the more profitable dividend income becomes in your portfolio. In fact, in the long term, dividend payments over a one-year period can surpass the amount you actually invested in the stock. After a 20 year period, for instance, you could be receiving a dividend of $100,000 a year in a stock for which you only paid $100,000. You would therefore be receiving all the money you paid for that stock every year in dividends alone.

Various companies, especially those recently established or new to the stock exchange, may not pay dividends. Companies that do not pay dividends may often do so either because they believe their earnings are low or that a better use of after tax profits is to reinvest in the business for further growth. The portion of a company's after tax profits kept for the future development of the business and not shared as dividends with investors is referred to as retained earnings.

Older, larger companies may however pay dividends on a consistent basis as they have already grown their businesses so significantly that it may be difficult for them to find new opportunities for growth. They may therefore decide to share a large part of their earnings with shareholders in the form of dividends. Large companies that consistently pay dividends include companies like **Carreras Limited, GraceKennedy Group, NCB Financial Group, Scotia Group Jamaica Limited, Jamaica Broilers Group, Sagicor Group Jamaica Limited and PanJam Investment Limited.** As smaller companies grow, they may also distribute dividends to shareholders over time.

A company also has the option of paying its dividends in the form of shares and may therefore opt for a bonus issue of shares. This occurs when a company converts its reserves into shares and distributes these to existing shareholders in proportion to the shares they currently own. Cash dividends are, however, the most common form of dividend paid.

There are several key dates to bear in mind. When a dividend is announced, the announcement includes an X-Date, a Record Date and a Payment Date. You will not be entitled to receive the announced dividend if you become an owner of the stock on or after the X-Date or the ex-dividend date. To receive the announced dividend you must own the stock before the X-Date.

The Record Date is the date on which the record of shareholders is examined in order to determine which shareholders were owners of the stock before the X-Date and therefore would be entitled to a dividend. In order for investors to earn a dividend, they must be shareholders at the Record Date; that is, an investor must appear on the company's share register by this date to be entitled to receive dividends or bonuses. This is usually a day or two after the Ex-Date. Selling your shares after the Record Date does not affect your entitlement to a dividend as you would already have been recorded as entitled to the dividend on the Record Date.

The Payment Date is the date on which the dividend is paid to the shareholders who were recorded as being shareholders on the Record Date.

Dividends may be paid by a company by sending a cheque to the investor. In some cases because the total dividends appear to the investor to be small amounts, they may simply not be bothered to go to the bank to deposit them. This is a mistake as dividends add up over time. In order to avoid this, you can go in to your broker and complete a dividend mandate form instructing the registrar of the company whose stock you own to deposit your dividends directly to your bank account. This avoids the risk that your cheques may get lost in the mail or that you end up never encashing them. This is the most convenient way to ensure you receive all your dividends. This approach is strongly encouraged.

## Price Appreciation

In addition to dividends, you can benefit from an increase in the price of the share you purchased. As the demand for the share increases, other investors become willing to pay more for each share of the company. Those investors who bought the share at a lower price therefore see the value of their investment increase as the share price increases. The forces of supply and demand are therefore important in determining whether stock prices appreciate. The number of shares issued by a company puts a cap on the availability of shares for that company. As new investors try to buy shares from those investors who own the finite number of issued shares, the buyer may have to pay more in order to purchase those shares from the seller. The price of the share increases as demand for it grows, and it becomes more and more valuable to potential investors.

Although dividend payments from larger companies are very important, most of the gains from stock investing often come from the appreciation in the price of stocks over time. Smaller companies are more likely to experience faster stock price increases over time because they may have much more potential to grow. Larger more established companies may have already grown so significantly that there is not much more room for growth. This is not an unbreakable rule, however. In some cases large companies with great management teams and a good business model grow at extraordinary rates. NCB Financial Group, for instance, has been one of the largest and most profitable companies in Jamaica.

However, despite its size, it has grown significantly, even outpacing the growth of smaller companies. As a result, the stock price of NCB grew from $73 in mid July 2017 to some $214 in mid July 2019. That represents a price appreciation of over 190 per cent in two years. Much of this reflected the company's rapid expansion by acquiring stakes in other profitable companies in the Caribbean. A small or medium sized company may not therefore always be a faster grower than a large company. Each company must be assessed individually to determine its potential for growth and, by extension, the potential for its stock price to appreciate over time.

## What is a Stock Split?

From time to time companies may decide to split their stock. When a company splits its stock, it divides its total number of shares into a larger number of shares without changing the company's total capitalization. Capitalization refers to the total value of the company as measured by the total number of shares multiplied by the price of each share. When a company decides to split its stock, it first determines the ratio. For instance, it may decide to split at a ratio of 2:1. If each stock was worth $10 before the split, that stock would be split into two stocks, each worth $5. The total value of your investment would therefore remain the same, even though you have more stocks. After the stock split, an investor who had 10 stocks worth $100 would therefore now have 20 stocks worth the same $100.

In this scenario, if the company had 1 million outstanding shares before the spilt, it would have 2 million outstanding shares after the split worth the same dollar value as the initial 1 million shares. Companies sometimes split their stock in order to make them more affordable thus increasing demand for the stock from investors. Apart from making the shares more affordable, stock splits do not fundamentally change anything else. For instance, it does not mean that the company will earn more money or be more profitable. Buying a stock simply because the company has announced a split therefore may not mean much for the investor in the long term. However, many investors like the idea of stock splits and often try to buy the stock before it splits. This increased demand often increases the price of the stock before the split. As noted above, however, nothing fundamentally changes in relation to the future profitability of the company simply because of a stock split.

## Initial Public Offerings (IPOS)

An Initial Public Offering or an IPO occurs when a private company first offers its shares to the public for purchase. Private companies arrange IPOs to raise capital to build their businesses. In an IPO, the private company engages the services of a stock brokerage company to organize and manage the issuance of the shares. The stock brokerage company advertises a prospectus that is the legal document explaining the IPO to the public, including information on the company and instructions to the public on how to apply for shares. The Jamaica Stock Exchange website always advertises this information at www.jamstockex.com.

IPOs often present excellent opportunities to buy a company's shares. Often the share prices of those companies rise significantly after their IPOs. This may occur because the public views the company as a good company with potential to grow. The number of shares a company offers to the public may also be small compared to the high demand for those shares. In that case, investors who were unable to obtain all the shares they applied for at the IPO may attempt to buy them when the stock starts to trade on the market thus driving up demand and the share price. Investors who are able to buy shares during the IPO may therefore see massive returns on their investment in a relatively short period.

The Jamaica Stock Exchange has seen excellent examples of this in recent years. Good examples are **Indies Pharma Jamaica Limited (Indies) and Stationery and Office Supplies Limited (SOS).** In July 2017, Stationery and Office Supplies Limited (SOS) made an initial public offering of shares at $2.00 each. As at November 2018, those shares were worth over $9.00. An investor who bought shares in SOS at its IPO would therefore have made some 350% on his investment in less than one and a half years. In the case of **Indies Pharma**, the shares were offered at an IPO price of $1.50 in July 2018. By November 2018, less than 6 months after **Indies Pharma** became a listed company on the Jamaica Stock Exchange, its share price rose to $3.00. Investors in the IPO would therefore have gained 100% on their investment in 4 months. Not all IPOs are as successful. Therefore, investors wishing to invest in IPOs should read the company's prospectus carefully and seek advice from their registered financial advisers on whether the company issuing an IPO is a good investment.

I will give some general guidance in the next chapter on how to select the best stocks for investment. Some of these principles are also applicable to the selection of IPOs.

## How to Buy Shares in an IPO

When a private company announces that it will offer shares in an IPO, it must, in conjunction with its broker, issue a prospectus. You should read a copy of the prospectus before investing.

If you are interested in buying shares in an IPO you should:
- Obtain and read a copy of the company prospectus;
- Seek advice from an investment adviser;
- Complete the subscription for shares form at the end of the prospectus or use an electronic platform such as NCB's GoIPO if the shares can be purchased on that platform;
- If a paper application form is completed, submit either to the Lead Broker arranging the IPO or your own stockbroker the completed subscription form along with any accompanying documents such as identification and TRN;
- Make payment for the shares as instructed in the prospectus; and
- Ensure that all documents are submitted and payments made before the opening date of the IPO as stated in the prospectus.

Where an electronic platform such as NCB's GoIPO is used, payment for the shares must comply with the requirements stated on the GoIPO platform. The platform allows for payment by RTGS or other electronic means or by deducting funds from an NCB account or via cheque.

You should take special note of the opening and closing dates of IPOs. The closing date is often simply an indicative date. The Lead Broker arranging the IPO may decide to close the offer before the closing date. There is no guarantee that an offer will remain open until its closing date; it may become oversubscribed and in fact close mere minutes after it is open. You should therefore submit your application before the opening date.

## How to Buy and Sell Listed Stocks on the JSE

If you wish to buy or sell stocks already listed on the stock exchange you must do so through a stockbroker. The process is simple. You simply need to open a stock trading account with a stockbroker of your choice, deposit funds to the account and instruct the broker to purchase the stocks you wish to hold. In some cases the broker may have an app or an online platform which allows you to place the instruction/make the order electronically. On receiving such an instruction, the broker places an order at the JSE. The Stock Exchange then matches that order to an investor who wishes to sell his shares in that company and executes the transaction. Those shares are then considered purchased by the broker on your behalf. The Jamaica Central Securities Depository (JCSD) then records the purchase. In the case of a sale of stocks, the broker also acts on your instructions, whether electronic or otherwise, by offering your shares for sale on the market.

The stockbroker works to get the best price for the investor. The broker also provides investment advice and plays the role of an agent or intermediary between you and the stock exchange. Every investor should use a broker to buy or sell shares and each broker must be in possession of a member/dealer licence approved by the Board of the JSE in order to trade on the stock exchange. In addition to holding a trading licence, the stock brokering firm must be in a good financial state and meet certain financial requirements on a continual basis.

There are several stockbrokers in Jamaica which are licensed to purchase and sell stocks on behalf of individual investors. You may choose the broker you prefer or most trust. Before selecting a broker, you should get as much information as possible about the broker. You may visit the stockbroker's office, and speak to a representative to get an idea of the type of service offered.

You may also speak with other investors about their experiences with particular brokers. You may decide on a single broker or more than one broker depending on your needs. If you are investing small sums, then a single broker would be fine. Without being exhaustive, the list of brokers in Jamaica includes:

**Mayberry Investments Ltd.**
1 1/2 Oxford Road
Kingston 5
Tel: 876-929-1908-9
www.mayberryinv.com

**Jamaica Money Market Brokers (JMMB)**
Head Office
6 Haughton Terrace
Kingston 10
Tel: 876-960-9546
www.jmmb.com

## NCB Capital Markets Ltd.
Head Office
The Atrium
32 Trafalgar Road
Kingston 10
Tel: 876-960-7108
www.ncbcapitalmarkets.com

## GK Capital Management
58 Hope Road
Kingston 6
Tel: 876-932-3290
Email: GKCapital@gkco.com
www.gk-capital.com

## Scotia Investments Jamaica Ltd.
Tel: 1-888-429-5745

## Stocks and Securities Ltd.
Head Office
33 1/2 Hope Road
Kingston 10
Tel: 876-929-3400
www.sslinvest.com

## Victoria Mutual Wealth Management
53 Knutsford Boulevard
Kingston 5
Tel: 876-960- 5000-3
Email: info@vmwealth.com
www.vmwealth.vmbs.com

## Sagicor Investments Ltd.
Head Office
85 Hope Road
Kingston
Tel: 876-929-8920
www.sagicorjamaica.com

## JN Fund Managers Ltd.
2 Belmont Road
Kingston 5
Tel: 876-929-2289
Email:info@jnfunds.com
www.jnfunds.com

## Barita Investments Ltd.
Head Office
15 St. Lucia Way
Kingston 5
Tel: 876-926-2681/926-6673
www.barita.com

## Proven Wealth Management Ltd.
Head Office
26 Belmont Road
Kingston 5
Tel: 876-908-3800
www.provenwealth.com

## M/VL Stockbrokers Ltd.
19 Holborn Road
Kingston 10
Tel: 876-926-4319
www.mvl.com.jm

## BCW Capital
82 Knutsford Boulevard
Kingston 5
Tel: 876-754-2291

## Services to be Expected of Your Stock Broker

Your brokerage firm executes your orders to buy or sell shares on your behalf. Your broker should also advise you of the stock orders which have been filled. Some firms do this by email. Brokers also provide investment advice and research material on stocks either on your request or on their own initiative. They also keep a record of your stock holdings and your account balances and market transactions. You should therefore ensure that you capitalize on all the services that your broker offers. This will help to ensure greater success as you navigate the market.

## What to Consider When Choosing Your Broker

There are a few basic things you should consider when choosing a broker. You should consider how accessible your broker will be. Some brokers allow you to place an order by sending them an email once you sign an email indemnity form. Some brokers allow you to place orders online on a dedicated electronic platform. This is an easy option if, for instance, you don't want to have to go into your broker's office to place an order or if you are overseas and want to purchase or sell shares.

You may also consider how user friendly a broker's online trading platform is. In addition, you could consider the quality and amount of analysis they provide on individual stocks to guide their clients and the quality of investment advice they are willing to provide. You also may wish to consider brokers who show patience with new investors and who are willing to guide you through the investing process at your pace. Those brokers that take time and attention to sit with you and listen to your investment goals while working out a strategy that suits your needs are good choices. Another consideration are brokers' fees or commissions compared to other brokers. The lower a broker's fees are, the less likely fees will decrease your returns over the long term.

## Practical Considerations When Trading Stocks

### Market Orders

When purchasing or selling stocks, you have the option of choosing a market order or instructing your broker to enter a limit order. Where you choose a market order, the stock will be bought or sold at the price at which it is trading on the market at the moment the order is executed. There are advantages and disadvantages to selecting a market order. One disadvantage is that you have no control over the stock's buying or selling price. You are left to the mercy of the market.

If you are purchasing at the market price, the market price of the stock at the time you find a willing seller could be significantly more than you anticipated. These price movements may be temporary, so with a market order, you may end up buying a stock at a higher price than anticipated. Soon after you buy, the price could fall significantly, resulting in an immediate loss. That is the risk a purchaser takes when purchasing at market price. In the same scenario, the seller who enters a market order has no control over the price at which his shares will be sold. They may be sold at a lower price than he anticipated or a higher price, depending on the forces of demand

and supply. Buying or selling shares at market price therefore results in significant uncertainty and is a risk the stockholder takes.

## Limit Orders

A limit order gives you a greater degree of control than a market order. With a limit order, you set the price at which you are willing to sell or purchase a stock. The order will not be executed until the market price of the stock hits your limit price. By setting a limit price, therefore, you do not run the risk of purchasing a stock at a higher price than you would have liked, nor would sellers end up selling at a lower price than their ideal price. The disadvantage with a limit order, however, is that it takes a longer time to sell or purchase your stock as you must wait until the market price becomes the same as the limit price you have set. When you set a limit price, you also run the risk of making unrealistic predictions about where the stock price will move.

For example, if you set a limit price that is too low, hoping to buy the stock at a bargain, you run the risk of the order never being executed as the market price may never fall to the low limit price. On the other hand, if you set too high a selling price you may also end up being unable to sell as the market price never rises to this limit price. Patient investors who are willing to wait until the market price moves to their limit price, however, may reap the rewards in the long term if they are able to buy cheap and sell dear.

## Minimum Purchases

The JSE has set a limit of a minimum of 100 shares for any purchase of stock in a company. You must therefore ensure that you purchase a minimum of 100 shares in any company in which you wish to invest.

## Limit Periods

When placing a stock order, you may need to indicate how long the order will remain valid. This may vary from one day to one month. An unfilled order expires at the end of the limit period and must be resubmitted if you still wish to have it executed.

In some cases you could instruct your broker to keep the order valid until it is executed or until you issue further instructions.

## Brokerage Commissions

Both buyers and sellers of stocks are generally required to pay a fee or commission to the broker. The broker's fee is generally about 2 per cent of the gross value of a transaction over $20,000.

Many brokers set a minimum commission of between $200 and $500, depending on the broker, for transactions below $20,000. Transactions below $20,000 may therefore, as a percentage of the value of shares, result in higher brokerage costs. Transactions over $20,000 may therefore be more cost effective.

## The Jamaica Central Securities Depository (JCSD) Trade Fee

You are also required to pay a JCSD trade fee. The fee as of October 2018, which could be subject to change in the future, is three (3) basis points of the value on each side of the trade.

This means that the cost for each order will be based on the value of that trade and the cost of the transaction will be based on the value despite the number of trades required to fill the order.

## The Settlement Period

As of December, 2017, the Jamaica Stock Exchange and the JCSD settle stock sale and purchase transactions two days after the date of trade. This means that all payments to an investor and transfers of shares in a sale or purchase transaction are completed two days after the transaction is executed. The new settlement period that has been reduced from three days, reflects international standards.

## JCSD Accounts

Before trading in shares your broker will open a JCSD account on your behalf. The JCSD is a subsidiary of the Jamaica Stock Exchange and its role is to hold securities such as stocks by keeping a record of stock ownership or sale by each investor. It allows shares to change ownership electronically between parties. Unlike previously, investors who buy stocks no longer need a share certificate as evidence of ownership of the shares as this is reflected in their JCSD account. You can obtain information on how many shares you own in a company from the JCSD. The JCSD also issues statements of your accounts.

One important factor to consider is whether you wish to buy shares only in your name or jointly with another individual such as a family member. Where you purchase shares jointly, you will be assigned a joint JCSD account. Once your broker opens the JCSD account on your behalf, this information cannot change. All transactions relating to shares owned jointly must obtain the written consent of all joint owners. You must therefore carefully consider whether it is convenient to open a joint account as all parties may not be available at the same time to consent to certain transactions on the account.

### How Much do you Need to Start?

You need not have large sums of money to start investing in stocks. A few thousand dollars are sufficient to start. Stockbrokers require varying minimum amounts to open an account. You should consult your preferred broker for advice. It is important however to add to your investment as time progresses.

Money that you need for immediate expenses such as food, rental and transportation should not be invested in stocks as stock investing is a long-term exercise. The shorter your time horizon, the more likely you will be forced to sell stocks at a loss to meet basic expenses if you do not have enough time to wait for the price to recover.

## When not to Invest in the Stock Market

### When you are Indebted

Persons who are deeply in debt, whether by way of credit card debt or otherwise, should not generally invest in stocks. Buying stocks when you owe money that you have difficulty repaying is never prudent. A return on your stock investment of 11% would never outpace the 19% interest on your debt, for example. My advice to the prospective investor is first to pay down debt before even thinking of investing in the stock market.

**When You Need to Spend the Money You Have Invested in the next 5 years**

You should never invest money that you need in the next five years in the stock market. If you need the money for any reason, whether to pay for groceries, health insurance, tuition, transportation or any other immediate or medium term necessity, it should never enter the stock market. This is because it may take at least five years for you to earn a decent return on your investment. Stock investing is a long-term exercise. Selling your investments before at least five years could lead to significant losses if the market or the stocks in which you invest fall in value shortly after you invest.

While some investors may prefer to trade stocks by buying and selling over short periods in order to take advantage of quick spikes in a stock price, this approach tends to be less successful than holding good stocks for the long run.

**When you do not fully understand Stocks or the Stock Market**

You should avoid the market before you have learned enough to understand stocks. Putting money into the stock market before you have a good grasp of it amounts to irresponsible speculation.

# How to Read the Stock Tables

At the end of each trading day, the Jamaica Stock Exchange produces a stock chart or quote sheet like in the table below. As confusing as the numbers look, they are quite simple once you understand how to read the chart.

I have attempted to set out below how you should read the charts as it is a useful piece of information that should assist in informing decision-making.

| Security | Last Traded Price (Jmd) | Close Price (Jmd) | Price Change (Jmd) | Closing Bid | Closing Ask | Volume | Today's High | Today's Low |
|---|---|---|---|---|---|---|---|---|
| BRG | 18.00 | 18.00 | -0.62 | 18.00 | 18.95 | 40,000 | 18.50 | 17.95 |

Security (BRG):   This is the symbol used to identify the company. In this case, the company is Berger Paints Jamaica Limited.

Last traded price:   The last price at which BRG traded during the trading day was $18.00.

Close price:   The price at which BRG closed at the end of the trading day was $18.00.

Price change:   Is the difference between the close price the stock traded on the previous day and the current close price. Therefore, the stock traded 62 cents lower than the previous day.

Closing bid:   $18.00 was the highest price an investor was willing to pay for BRG shares at the end of the day.

Closing ask:    $18.95 was the lowest price at which a seller was willing to sell BRG shares at the end of the trading day.

Volume:    The total volume of shares of BRG traded on the market at the end of the trading day.

Today's high:    During the trading day, BRG traded for as much as $18.50.

Today's low:    During the trading day, BRG traded for as low as $17.95.

| Security | 52 Week High (Jmd) | 52 Week Low (Jmd) | Pre. Yr. Div. | Current Yr. Div. | Yield |
|---|---|---|---|---|---|
| BRG | 24.00 | 14.55 | 0.50 | 0.28 | 2.5% |

52 week high:    The highest price paid for the stock in the past year was $24.00.

52 week low:    The lowest price paid for the stock in the past year was $14.55.

Prev. yr. div.:    The dividend paid on each stock in the previous year was 50 cents.

Current yr. div.:      The dividend paid on each share so far this year is 28 cents.

Yield:   The dividend per share represents 2.5% of the stock price (2.5% in this instance is hypothetical).

You therefore earned 2.5% dividend during the last year on the total value of your investment in BRG.

## The Environment that Influences Stocks

The stock market and stock prices fluctuate over time. This is partly because the market operates in an environment that may impact on the value of companies. First, the state of the national economy has an important effect on stocks. As national economies improve and employment increases, nationals have more money to buy goods and services. Companies supplying those goods and services become more profitable. Lower national debt levels also free up financing for private sector companies to expand and grow profits. This also tends to have a positive effect on the price of those companies' shares.

Certain economic indicators result in an ideal economic environment for stocks. These include the rate of growth of the economy. The faster the economy grows, the more prosperous companies tend to be and the more their stock prices increase. Investors should therefore be aware of the Gross Domestic Product or GDP that measures the size of the economy and how it grows over time.

The level of inflation in the economy or the consumer price index may also have an effect. As inflation falls, goods and services become less expensive and consumers spend less for the same goods and services. This allows them to save and invest more of their income. These greater investment levels tend to increase the demand for shares and result in stock price increases over time. The reverse is also true. Higher levels of inflation may dampen savings and investment levels and negatively affect the stock market because investors have to spend more of their income on basic goods and services.

Unemployment rates are also important. The lower the unemployment rate, the greater the percentage of the population that has jobs. As more people gain employment, demand for goods and services increases, thus increasing the profitability of companies and their stock prices.

The level of interest rates may also affect the growth of the stock market and the profitability of individual stocks. As interest rates on government paper, such as treasury bills fall, stocks become a more attractive investment. Investors generally look for investments that yield the highest returns. Therefore, as interest rates fall, stocks tend to yield higher returns than other types of investments that yield progressively lower interest rates.

Consumer and business confidence can also have an impact on the stock market. As consumers and businesses become more positive about the future of the economy, they become more willing to invest. As they invest and expand, profits increase and returns on shares rise for investors. The higher business and consumer confidence grow, the more likely it is that investments will also increase in value.

The state of the world economy and developments in global politics may also affect the stock market. As the size of the global economy fell during the 2008 global financial crisis, for example, many consumers earned less or lost their jobs and demand for goods and services fell globally. Local companies that exported overseas saw the demand for their exports fall resulting in lower profits and lower share prices.

The global crisis may also have negatively affected persons sending money home to their family in Jamaica, leading to fewer remittances and consequently less money available for family in Jamaica to buy goods and services. This also naturally led to reduced sales for local companies and lower share prices. The state of the global economy, therefore, can have a direct impact on the state of the Jamaican economy and, by extension, the stock market.

Global or regional political developments can also have an impact on the market indirectly. A political dispute between, for example, the United States and an oil producing country could lead to a fall in the supply of oil on the global market and a consequent increase in global oil prices.

As oil prices increase, it becomes more costly for local companies to produce. By paying more for electricity as a result of high oil prices, a company may see a fall in profits and a consequent reduction in its share price over time. Investors should therefore keep abreast not only of national developments but international developments and analyse their potential impact on the stock market.

Company and industry trends also affect overall stock prices. A company forms part of an industry. The **Wisynco Group**, for example, is part of the manufacturing industry, while **Jamaica Money Market Brokers** is part of the financial industry. The general performance of an industry can have implications for individual stocks in that industry.

A general downturn in the manufacturing industry affecting all companies in that industry could cause the price of the stock you own in that industry to fall. For example, higher oil prices may increase the cost of manufacturing thus lowering the profits of **Wisynco** along with all other companies in the manufacturing industry. Keeping abreast of developments in an industry can therefore be very important in deciding when to buy or sell a stock or whether to hold it for the long run.

## Where to Find Information on Listed Companies

You will notice as you read this book that there is an emphasis on the stock picker doing his own meticulous research. Research is one of the most important aspects of stock investing. You must dedicate a good deal of time to it in order to fully understand the companies you invest in before you buy a single share.

Good sources of information on a listed company can be found in its quarterly and annual reports that are published on the Jamaica Stock Exchange website. Other sources of information you should consider are newsletters and analyses from your stockbroker.

Some of this information may be available on your stockbroker's website. You may also consider speaking directly with your broker on companies whose stocks you are interested in purchasing. Their research departments may have useful data to share that will help you to select the best stocks. Most brokers will be happy to provide you with that information. It is also important to learn to read and understand the company's financial statements but also other financial publications that may have information relevant to the company's business.

Newspaper publications also have useful information. You should therefore keep abreast of the business section of local newspapers as an alternative source of information.

## The Risks of Investing in Stocks

Stock market investing, like most investments, involves risk. While stock prices tend to increase over the long term, the prices of shares can fall, even dramatically. This could lead to losses for an investor. You should bear in mind that stock market fluctuations are normal. Companies vary in how well they do over time.

A company that does well by increasing earnings and revenue may also, from time to time, face challenges and perform badly over one or several quarters. This may result in share price declines and investment losses for the investor. Global and national economic conditions can also affect the performance of companies.

As the global or national economy declines, stock prices of companies may fall resulting in losses for the investor.

The risk of investor sentiment is also important to bear in mind. Investors may become negative about the economy or a particular company even if the long-term fundamentals of the company are good. In those cases, share prices may also fall, resulting in losses for the investor.

Investors who hold good companies for the long term, however, need not be very concerned about short-term downturns in their company's stock price. As we discussed earlier, over the long term, stock prices tend to move upwards and outpace other forms of investment. The longer you hold the shares of great companies, therefore, the less you need to worry about short term reductions in share prices.

# Notes

[18] Seprod Annual Report 2016 page 30- Report of Chairman P.B. Scott.
[19] Seprod 2016 Annual Report page 29.

# THE ESSENTIAL COMMANDMENTS OF STOCK INVESTING

Create the Goals You Hope to Achieve Before Investing
Research
Find Well Managed Companies
Find the Industry Leader
Don't Be Overconfident
Stick to What You Know
Resist Fads
Minimize Speculation
Look for Growing Companies
Look for Growth
Select Companies with Consistent Annual Dividend Increases
Take Advantage of Opportunities
Sell When Overpriced or When the Business is Declining
Have Reasonable Expectations
Reinvest all Dividends
Diversify (Industry and Size) (Large, Medium and Small Cap Stocks)
Invest Regularly
Buy at a Reasonable Price
Buy and Hold
Control Leverage
Be Patient
Ignore the Stock Price
Ignore the Market
Ignore Tips
Look for Companies with Good Finances
Don't Overinvest
Don't Be Fooled by Past Performance
Favour Limit Orders
Control Your Emotions
Keep doing Your Homework

# THE ESSENTIAL COMMANDMENTS OF STOCK INVESTING

**"All you need for a lifetime of investing are a few big winners"**
- Peter Lynch.

Successful stock selection is far from being an overwhelming exercise. Wise investors follow a logical formula by using a predictable method to separate the wheat from the chaff. If investors proceed without a compass, driven by elusive promises of unrealistically high returns, rather than a sound approach that is logical, rational and tempered by realistic expectations, they will be unsuccessful.

The good news is that stock investing simply requires adhering to sound principles. I call them **the essential commandments of stock investing.** Anyone who uses those principles well can succeed. Because principles matter, Warren Buffett once said, *"You don't need to be a rocket scientist. Investing is not a game where the guy with the 160 IQ beats the guy with the 130 IQ".* As a beginning non-professional investor, I found that advice to be pivotal. It reassured me that investing, even in stocks, is not as complex as it is often thought to be. Stock investing can in fact be simple and enjoyable. All you have to do is practice basic disciplines and execute a rational strategy. Those basic principles are so obvious and so simple that investors often overlook them. In fact, most investors lack the discipline to apply them.

So the following are outlines of some of the basic principles. Anyone may use these principles to select the best companies for a long-term investment portfolio.

## Create the Goals You Hope to Achieve Before Investing

You should first determine why you are investing in stocks and must set specific goals so that you can frame your strategies to meet those goals. If you are investing for financial security in retirement, then your investment timeline and strategy should align to that goal. In that case, you should make specific calculations at the outset as to the amount of money you would need in order to retire comfortably.

There are many ways to do this as there is no lack of websites and financial advisers who can recommend the ideal figure. One basic rule of thumb is to calculate your annual living expenses and multiply them by 25. So if the investor's annual living expenses amount to $2,500,000, the investor's targeted saving for retirement should at least be $62,500,000. This may sound like an unachievable target but as we continue, you will discover that this target is possible for almost any disciplined investor as long as he or she adopts a wise investment strategy. When you hit your target, you may generally safely retire and begin to withdraw 4 per cent per annum from your savings, provided your principal continues to be invested and yields a return of over 4 per cent. This, however, comes with a caveat. You should bear in mind that for this rule to work, your investment must be earning more than the rate of inflation. Under no circumstances should you withdraw more than 4 per cent per annum. At this rate of withdrawal, your savings should last you throughout your retirement, provided you are earning enough on your investment to take account of inflation. This is the 4 per cent withdrawal rule that many financial experts suggest works 99 per cent of the time. Various online retirement calculators and formulas are also available and give other options on how wise investors may calculate their ultimate goals.

The 4 per cent rule, however, is a rule of thumb often used in the United States context with more or less stable rates of inflation and a stable currency. It is not a rule that is guaranteed to work in the Jamaican context. I recommend therefore that you not rely entirely on this rule but that you sit with your financial adviser who would be better able to guide you on the ideal amount you will need for retirement based on your individual circumstances.

By determining your long-term objectives, you can more easily develop the best strategy to reach those objectives. Irrespective of your objectives, it is critical, however, that you see stock investing as a key component. If you use stocks as a tool, your goals will inform how much capital you invest in the market. So, the longer your time horizon, the more you can invest in stocks. Shorter time horizons however would dictate less focus on stocks. Money needed in the next 6 months to five years should therefore not be part of your stock investment portfolio. This will ensure that you do not need to liquidate or sell shares if prices have fallen in order to recoup money for immediate expenses. By determining your goals at the outset, you can better tailor your approach to stock investing.

## Research

Nathan Mayer Rothschild, patriarch of arguably the most successful banking dynasty in the world, once said, "information is money." As a result of Rothschild's extensive network of carrier pigeons, specially employed couriers and informants, he learned that France had been defeated by England at the battle of Waterloo before any other investor in London became aware. As other investors were selling stocks in the expectation that Britain would lose, Rothschild was buying stocks heavily. Needless to say, when everyone else learned the news, his wealth exploded in value and his family became one of the richest families in the world in the 1800s, financing many European States on the brink of bankruptcy throughout the Napoleonic Wars. You should use the same approach when investing in stocks.

Most persons spend countless hours researching the latest clothing fashion, smart phones and luxury cars before they buy. They compare prices, brands and sizes in store and online, yet they spend little to no time researching their investments. Any investor who has not done his research should never buy stocks, no matter how attractive they may appear. In his book *"One Up on Wall Street: How to Use what You Already Know to Make Money in the Market"*, Peter Lynch underscored the importance of research. He correctly said that, *"it is personal preparation, as much as knowledge and research that distinguishes the successful stock picker from the chronic loser. Ultimately, it is not the stock market or even the companies themselves that determine an investor's fate. It is the investor.* " He also lamented that people spend months choosing their houses and minutes choosing their stocks.

To have the ultimate advantage, you must make research your primary task. You should draw your research from various independent sources. You therefore should not rely solely on newspaper and media reports on a company nor the research of financial experts, although these may guide you. You should make an effort to read as much information about the company, its areas of business, and its future plans as you possibly can. You may find much of this information in the company's quarterly financial reports and annual reports on the Jamaica Stock Exchange website. These reports contain a useful section where management gives a succinct summary of the most vital measures of the company's performance over the past quarter or year. It is from these reports that you can develop a clear picture of how the company has been performing and what its plans are for the future.

This information is useful in developing a good picture of whether the company you wish to invest in has been executing its development plan well and continues to be a prosperous business. These reports also contain the financial statements of the company that, for average investors, may be somewhat difficult to understand unless they have an accounting background.

Although you may rely on the summary report, you should also educate yourself on how to read these statements. This is a critical skill that pays dividends over time. Being able to read and understand a company's financial statements and measure the company's financial performance and business prospects over time gives the investor an edge in picking the companies with the greatest potential for growth. I therefore strongly recommend that every stock investor read books on investing and how to assess the performance of businesses. It is an article of faith that investment in financial education pays the biggest dividend of all. It keeps you from purchasing the wrong stock for the wrong reasons and from relying on the analysis of others. My advice, then, is that you never invest in a stock before you have done the most exhaustive research possible on the company.

## Find Well Managed Companies

The quality of a company's management is possibly one of the key determinants of its success. A good business that has visionary and competent leaders traditionally does excellently. Wise investors therefore invest in companies with managers who are driven by long-term growth and debt reduction and who are not focused on short-term stock price movements or investor demands.

You should therefore look for management with a good track record and a reputation for success in the industry. You should look for management that uses the company's cash to further build a business that is performing well. As attractive as dividends may be for shareholders, it would be sound management to reinvest the company's free cash in growing the business. You should therefore look for companies with management that allocates profits by not only paying dividends but by further investing in the company.

Warren Buffett is an ardent proponent of the ability to allocate capital as a hallmark of good management. His well-known view is that the best managers consistently invest cash in activities that will bring greater returns to the business. Managers who allocate capital well build shareholder value over time.

As part of your assessment of management quality, you should also look for companies with managers who devote themselves to sound strategic thinking and demonstrate rationally how the company will achieve its targets. You should therefore ensure that tested and proven management runs any company whose stocks you buy. Most of your information on management will inevitably come from company annual reports and news reports on company business policy of which you must always keep abreast.

## Find the Industry Leader

In every industry, a leader will emerge. Wise investors consistently look for that leader. Typically, the leader is the most recognized and the strongest company in the industry. It often enjoys superior market share compared to its competitors and has usually invested so heavily in building its business model and customer loyalty that few if any competitor would ever have the resources or skills to match its dominant position.

Another way for you to look at this principle is to find the company that has the highest sales and best quality product in its industry. If the company sells the most, it is highly likely to be the best of its class. Wise investors therefore look for the company that produces a product that people like and are willing to buy over its competitors' products. If the company maintains and improves the quality of its product or service, it is most likely going to make a lot of money in its industry and make its shareholders happy.

There are many obvious examples of companies that are industry leaders. We could first look at the manufacturing and banking sectors. Almost every Jamaican would agree that based on revenues and sales in these industries it is not hard to pick the leaders. **National Commercial Bank Financial Group (NCBFG)** reported annual profit of $28.6 billion in November 2018. This was the highest profit in the company's history, and the bank ranks in the top five in the Caribbean region in terms of pre-tax profits. In the manufacturing sector, an obvious industry leader is **GraceKennedy**. GraceKennedy has been a stalwart in the manufacturing sector with products of renowned quality.

We could also look at companies in the United States as examples of how to identify industry leaders. At the end of 2015, **Visa** enjoyed a 51.8 per cent market share. Its closest rival enjoyed only 30.2 per cent[20]. **Visa**, with its dominant market share, which it has maintained for years, is without doubt a classic industry leader. By this measure so is **Coca Cola**, which as of 2015 enjoyed a 42.5 per cent market share compared with its nearest rival with 25 per cent. One example in the growing field of e-commerce is **Amazon**. An analysis of 1.7 million online shopping receipts between 1st November and 16th December, 2016 showed Amazon had a 36.9 per cent share of the market compared to its nearest rival, Best Buy, with a 3.9 per cent share[21]. Visa, Coca Cola and Amazon also happen to be the dominant players in their industry with the best brand recognition and have had stable long-term success.

Most would agree that Coca Cola is and remains for the foreseeable future the dominant leader in the soda market. The company has built a position that is practically impossible for any other company to surpass. Coca Cola has built what Warren Buffett calls the "moat" which essentially conjures the image of ancient castles surrounded by wide, deep bodies of water. A moat historically gave castles extra protection from attack, as enemies had to reach the castle by sailing through the surrounding waters which made them easily detectable and vulnerable to defeat. Under the "moat" investing philosophy, some of the most desirable companies for investment are those that have so separated themselves from the competition that they will most likely remain unchallenged for the leadership role in their industry. These companies have built such a strong business brand or infrastructure or supply chain that their rivals would be unable to replicate it.

The above are simple but clear examples of how you can analyze a sector and make selections based on this criterion. However, in addition to superior sales and profits, the advantage of investing in the dominant player is that it has sufficient resources to weather downward pressures on the economy. Even in economically challenging times, nationally and globally, the dominant player has the best chance of surviving financial losses and profit declines while other less strong players that may be heavily indebted, could easily collapse or incur further massive debts and jeopardize their long-term profitability.

Let's look for examples at the United States for purposes of illustration. One example is the oil price collapse in 2015 that lasted well into 2016. Several small, heavily indebted oil exploration companies went out of business. An investment in those companies would have spelled disaster to a portfolio.

The big, dominant players in the oil industry like ExxonMobil, however, weathered the storm. It would be unthinkable to conceive an ExxonMobil collapse unless the world decided abruptly to stop consuming oil. In 2015 ExxonMobil was one of the largest multinational oil and gas companies in the world with an estimated market value of over US$356 billion. It was the second most profitable company in the Fortune 500 in 2014. Exxon and Mobil, before their merger, had a long history of success and had been around in previous incarnations since the 1800s. Over this long period, the company developed unparalleled expertise, assets and resources to stand the test of time. It has become perhaps the best known oil and gas company worldwide and few can challenge its dominance. The solidity of ExxonMobil's history and success ranks it among the most dominant players in the energy sector. No wonder it survived several oil price drops and continues to make profits year after year.

I use ExxonMobil, simply as an illustration of another good reason the investor should find the dominant player. The bonus is that they have a lower likelihood of failing.

Warren Buffett, who ranks among the most successful investors of all time, favours these kinds of companies. These are the companies that wise investors should also favor.

## Don't Be Overconfident

Overconfidence is a cognitive trait hard wired into the human brain. As a mental trait, overconfidence can persuade investors that they are more sophisticated investors than they really are. It lulls investors into taking uncalculated risks. They believe they can beat the market and make costly bets devoid of serious analysis.

Overconfidence leads would-be investors to restrict the information or facts they research or read in a way that confirms what they already believe. Such investors neglect, discredit or at best explain away information that contradicts or counters their beliefs.

Wise investors always guard against overconfidence. They do not overrate their abilities, knowledge or skill and temper their enthusiasm about any given stock investment. Wise investors do a "pre-mortem," an investment term coined by Professor Thomas Gilovich. That is, they distance themselves by considering the opposite side of a transaction before making it. They create a hypothetical scenario in which the investment fails and then consider how they should have foreseen that the investment was going to be a bad one. If there are sufficiently compelling reasons why the hypothetical scenario could occur they caution themselves against the investment.

## Stick to What You Know

There are dozens of publicly traded companies on the Jamaica Stock Exchange. You may be unfamiliar with some of those companies. Wise investors only invest in companies whose business they understand and whose future they can see. You should have a good idea of what the health of these companies would be like in ten years. In other words, you should limit yourself to those businesses that you can adequately analyze. When you know and understand a company, you are able to track its progress, and know when it is doing well or not and what its future looks like.

Warren Buffet famously justifies his investments in companies based on his ability to understand what they do. It is no wonder that among his largest holdings is Coca Cola. For Mr. Buffett, nobody has to explain what Coca Cola does or has to explain its products. Investing in Coca Cola therefore fits his philosophy. He invests in companies like Coca Cola because he can make a reasonably intelligent guess of how it will do in the future. This is because he understands exactly what the company does. Mr. Buffett has not invested in certain technology companies like Microsoft or Oracle because he does not understand their business and has no way of knowing if they will remain dominant in their fields in ten years. Because Mr. Buffett does not understand the details of technology, he stays away from investing in it because the sector is so competitive that new entrants and fast technology developments could displace companies overnight without him being aware.

As Mr. Buffett once said, *"I can understand [Coca Cola]… Anyone can understand [it]… It's a simple business…So I want a simple business, easy to understand, great economics now, honest and able management, and then I can see about in a general way where they are going to be ten years from now. And if I can't see where they are going to be ten years from now, I don't want to buy them."*

Good examples of companies that wise investors can easily understand are household name companies whose products they see or use on a daily basis. Good solid consumer brand companies almost always turn out to be good investments. No doubt, any investor is well aware of **GraceKennedy**, **Lasco Manufacturing**, **Wisynco** (producer of the popular WATA) and **Seprod**. Very few Jamaicans can avoid using products from these companies on a weekly or daily basis. These are brands that investors know and are just some examples of well-known companies that investors may consider.

## Resist Fads

When everyone begins to sing the praises of a specific hot stock and starts buying wildly, it is highly likely that you are too late to the party. When the gardener, the taxi driver and the store owner down the street are rushing in, wise investors should probably be rushing out. Euphoria is most likely a sign that a stock has become overvalued and is preparing for a nasty fall. Warren Buffett summarized the attitude of the wise investor in these circumstances when he said, *"be fearful when others are greedy…."*

Avoiding the herd mentality is one of the most vital disciplines of wise stock investors. They do not make decisions based on the opinions of relatives, neighbors or friends. In the United States, the dotcom stock market bubble between 1995 and 2001 was a classic example. It was a period of frenzied investments in technology and internet stocks. The high school teacher, the gardener, the electrician and grandma and grandpa all plunged into hot technology stocks. The prices for those stocks rose exponentially, and investors poured money into them feverishly. Large numbers of the highly sought after internet companies promptly collapsed by 2001, leaving investors in a tailspin. Those that did not collapse saw their stock prices falling over eighty per cent in some instances.

The dotcom bubble is simply one example of the consequences of being lured into frenzied market fads. You should guard against this temptation.

## Minimize Speculation

Wise investors acknowledge that building value in the stock market must involve a level of speculation. They know, however, that they should never confuse speculation with investing so they must strictly manage speculation.

They must minimize it and be prepared for volatility and loss where speculative stock selections are part of their portfolio. Speculative stocks tend to be young companies that appear to have potential but have not yet proved they can make sustainable profits. Speculation can generate significant profit or major loss, and wise investors try to reduce the risk of loss by extensively researching those speculative stocks.

For speculative stocks, especially young companies, there is a limit to the amount of information available for proper analysis. However, wise investors do all they can to gather all relevant data. They also ensure that only a small percentage of their portfolios contain speculative stocks. The younger they are, the more they can afford to expose a larger proportion of their portfolio to speculation. However young you are, though, speculative stocks should account for at the most 10 per cent of your portfolio.

The rule of thumb is that you should only speculate with the amount of money that you can afford to lose. In fact, you may be better off holding separate accounts for speculating on small amounts of money. You should never intermingle this money with your serious investing portfolio, and you should limit the funds you place in this account and never add to it out of temptation when things are going well.

Wise investors know that they must distinguish investment from speculation. They are well aware that by speculating, they should not delude themselves into thinking that they are actually investing. You should therefore keep speculative activities constantly in perspective.

## Look for Growing Companies, not only older blue chip companies

While I caution against speculation, I will also admit that wisely selected, small, growth companies can have a significantly positive effect on the investor's portfolio. These should not be ignored. Peter Lynch, one of the greatest investors of all time, put the matter this way: *"The size of a company has a great deal to do with what you can expect to get out of the stock…Specific products aside, big companies don't have big stock moves. In certain markets, they perform well, but you'll get your biggest moves in smaller companies. You don't buy stock in a giant such as Coca Cola expecting it to quadruple your money in two years."*[22]

Growth companies are those that are growing revenue, earnings or profits by double digits annually. These are often young companies or small and medium sized companies most of which are listed on the Junior Stock Exchange.

The advantage of carefully selecting those small and medium sized companies growing at a fast and sustainable pace is that many have significant potential. They can grow exponentially, lifting the fortunes of early investors. One only needs to consider a rather obscure unknown company like **Caribbean Flavours and Fragrances (CFF)** when it first issued its IPO. The company issued shares at its IPO at $2.25 in 2013. By December 2018, it was trading at $20. A $50,000 investment in the IPO would therefore be worth over $400,000 in 2018. The investor who bought the stock in its infancy would have seen more than 780 per cent return in 5 years and would be smiling all the way to the bank. What distinguishes a company like CFF from a mere speculative stock is the fact that it had been in existence years before its IPO as a profitable growing business. Its IPO was not the mark of its beginning as a company.

Investors who bought the stock would therefore have been able to assess how it had been performing as a business before its IPO and its potential for continued success. So the bigger the company, all things being equal, the slower it can be expected to grow, except for a few exceptional cases. Everything else being equal, smaller companies that are growing fast and have good financials and low debt are highly likely to lead to larger portfolio gains for wise investors. You therefore always ask yourself the question, **"where will future growth come from in this company?"** before investing. The clearer the evidence that there is current and future growth, the better the prospect of a successful investment. You should ask yourself the right questions about a company's future growth potential. As new information about increased earnings or expansion into new markets becomes available, investors should realize that there are better odds of success and should stay invested.

## Look for Growth

Growth is the Holy Grail for a successful stock investor. Growth simply means that over time the company is producing more, selling more of its products and earning more profits as seen from the company's sales, profits and earnings. The best investments with the highest potential for significant returns are most often in companies that are expanding their businesses sustainably without taking on unsustainable debt. Aggressive growers that find a way to offer better products and enter more and more markets outside of Jamaica have significant potential to grow wise investors' portfolios.

As companies grow, their stock prices follow. The faster companies grow without taking on unsustainable debt the higher their stock prices will go, all things being equal. The stock price may not rise in line with growth immediately.

It may take years. But as the market recognizes growth in the company, over time, the stock price of that company will generally grow in line with its earnings growth. This is why it is important that you keep an eye on the company's earnings. This is one of the most important indicators of where the stock price will likely go. As Peter Lynch stated, *"if you can follow only one bit of data, follow the earnings.[23]"* Stock prices follow earnings. As earnings grow, a company's stock price follows. Wise investors therefore always monitor how the company's earnings increase or decrease over time and make their investment decisions accordingly.

## Select Companies with Consistent Annual Dividend Increases

Dividend stocks lack excitement. They never fire the imagination like high growth stocks do. Yet dividend stocks can return great rewards to investors. Dividend investment is especially powerful because it allows you to compound your returns. Dividends are an easy way to make money whether you are retired and want consistent income or whether you still earn a salary.

Stocks with high dividend yields tend, over time, to do better than stocks with a low dividend or which do not pay dividends. You should therefore consider companies with consistent annual dividend growth for a special place in your portfolio. There are many sources of online information on companies that pay and increase dividends consistently. You should consult these sources, including various brokerage sites that produce weekly reports detailing various company data such as their annual dividend rate.

Some argue that dividend stocks are boring and even derisively refer to them as "grandma stocks" because of the preponderance of older people who buy those stocks that bring in an income during retirement. Yes, I admit that dividend stocks may not be as sexy as companies that grow at a much faster rate. High dividend stocks tend to grow much more slowly, and their stock prices tend to increase at a much slower rate; but they have several advantages. During down market periods when the stock market has sold off and stocks are in a prolonged rut, prospective wealth builders will still be earning money while they wait for prices to recover.

You should however be very discriminating when choosing dividend stocks. You should not automatically choose companies that pay high dividends as you should first consider several important factors. First, the fact that a company pays high dividends does not mean that the dividends may not be cut or suspended in the future, leaving you empty handed. The priority, then, should be to invest in those stocks you know well and understand and to invest in companies of high quality that have a proven track record of long term growth.

Look for companies that have been profitable over a long period of time.

You should also research the dividend payout ratio of a company before investing for dividends. The payout ratio is a measure of how much of the company's earnings and free cash flow are being paid out as dividends to investors. While it may be exciting to reward investors, a company that pays too much of its earnings and free cash flow to investors as dividends may be doing itself a disservice. The more of its earnings and free cash flow that a company keeps to reinvest, the more sustainable its ability to keep paying dividends. A company with high dividend yields and low payout ratios tends to yield greater annual returns over time.

For example, a company may be paying an attractively high 5 per cent dividend but its payout ratio is 80 per cent or 90 per cent of its earnings. In that case, it is only retaining 20 per cent or less for reinvestment; this may impede its ability to grow in the future and those high dividends may become unsustainable. The lower the payout ratio, the better and more sustainable its dividend. A payout ratio of less than 50 per cent is often a good sign.

When selecting the right dividend stocks for a portfolio, you should also favor those companies that are growing their earnings and free cash flow year after year. This gives the company the ability to keep paying dividends over time.

Companies that have a history of consistently increasing dividends annually are even better. Over time your returns from dividends will increase significantly if you remain invested in such companies. A quick search online can turn up very good lists of such companies. Good examples are **GraceKennedy**, **Carreras**, **Seprod**, **Salada Foods** and **Scotiabank Group**. These companies' dividends tend to be predictable and dependable, and there is usually little risk that they will discontinue dividend payments even during periods of economic crisis, inflation, oil price hikes or any such global economic or domestic shocks. The certainty gives you a greater level of security especially if you depend on dividends for a steady income.

An example of the advantage of dividend stocks over non-dividend paying stocks in the United States context is a good example that is also relevant to Jamaica when choosing to invest in dividend stocks over non-dividend paying stocks. Between 1991 and 2017, US$100,000 invested in the S&P 500 index would return 10.2 per cent annually leaving the investor with a little over US$1.4 million[24]. Yet the same US$100,000 invested in 17 solid dividend stocks (with dividends automatically reinvested) would have returned 13.8 per cent annually, leaving the same investor with a staggering US$3.2 million instead[25]. This example clearly illustrates the superiority of choosing great dividend paying stocks and automatically reinvesting the dividends.

There are other less lofty dividend payers that have paid dividends consistently over shorter periods which are worth considering. Some of those companies are just as prestigious and stable. They may be younger companies, but they have established a tradition of steady and reliable dividend payments over a long enough period. I would encourage the wise investor to also consider those companies carefully as, over time, they have the potential to grow dividends as much as the esteemed dividend stalwarts.

## Take Advantage of Opportunities

*"Opportunities come infrequently. When it rains gold, put out the bucket, not the thimble."*
                                                        - Warren Buffett.

When a good opportunity arises, make the best of it. The wise investor who consistently uses this strategy has a significant advantage. Opportunities present themselves in the stock market in various ways, whether through IPOs of already established profitable companies or through a significant drop in the stock price of a great company.

A significant drop in the price of a great company is rare but you should fully exploit this if it happens. After all, this strategy is the key advantage the most legendary investors have capitalized on. Warren Buffet himself summarizes the principle by saying, *"the best thing that happens to us is when a great company gets into temporary trouble…We want to buy them when they are on the operating table."*

However, before buying on such dips, you should do careful in-depth research to ensure that the bad news affecting a good company is not a sign of deeper troubles that have begun to surface. What may appear at first glance to be an opportunity may in fact be a death twitch. Before making any decision to take advantage of what appears to be an opportunity, you should therefore devote time to assessing the situation. You must first determine if the issues affecting the company are signs of further trouble to come.

Warren Buffett cautions the investor about being misled by a trap masquerading as an opportunity. In typical style, he frames a witty comment: *"In the world of business, bad news often surfaces serially: you see a cockroach in your kitchen; as the days go by, you meet his relatives."*

You must therefore approach apparent opportunities with caution. The most effective way of ensuring that an opportunity is in fact what it appears to be is to research the company and the apparent crisis in detail. Familiarity with the company's history, business model, quality of management and reputation often provide good indicators of whether the company will recover and whether an apparent crisis will be short lived.

I will use U.S. examples, as examples of Jamaican companies in crisis are not as well documented; but the principle remains the same for Jamaican companies. A classic U.S example is the **Coca Cola** crisis in mid-1999. Children in six schools in Belgium complained that the Coca Cola products they drank had a funny smell. They subsequently experienced severe headaches, vomiting and nausea and were hospitalized. The incident caused Governments in Belgium, France, the Netherlands and Luxembourg to ban Coca Cola products. Coca Cola was forced to recall 30 million cans and bottles of its products. The incident, naturally, caused a nightmare for the company and its reputation. Over 240 Belgian and French Citizens, especially school children, became ill mostly from Coke products manufactured at its Antwerp and Dunkirk plants. In its 113-year history, Coca Cola's 1999 product recall became the biggest it had ever overseen. Its response to the crisis was extremely poor and did further damage to the company's reputation. They tried to explain the crisis away, and the Coke executives handling the matter showed extreme insensitivity to the children, parents and customers involved. The reputational damage to the company worsened. The financial effects on Coke were even worse.

Its 1999 second-quarter net income fell by 21 per cent to US$942 million. The recall of its products cost Coca Cola Enterprises US$103 million. Revenues for the bottler fell by 5 per cent and its cash operating profit by 6 per cent.

Still, Coca Cola was, despite the crisis, a great company with a 113 year old history and a great future. From all indications, the company would eventually recover and continue to be a powerhouse in the beverage industry. This, for the prospective wealth builder in 1999, would have been a classic opportunity. A great company *"on the operating table"* as Warren Buffett put it. That would no doubt be a great example of the types of opportunities that investors should seize. Since June 30, 1999, the company has recovered and done very well. Coca Cola's crisis was clearly not an opportunity for investors to miss.

# Sell When Overpriced or When the Business is Declining

*"Should you find yourself in a leaking boat, energy devoted to changing vessels is likely to be more productive than energy devoted to patching leaks."*
- Warren Buffett

If someone is buying your car for $1,000,000 when it's worth $450,000 you take the money and run. The same obtains for a stock. A high price to earnings (P/E) ratio relative to other companies in the same sector may be a good indication to sell. The P/E ratio measures the ratio of a company's stock price to its earnings. A high P/E ratio often suggests that investors have overvalued a company. So while buy and hold continues to be an excellent strategy, it does not mean that you should never sell when the fundamental future prospects of a company get decidedly bad or when it becomes highly overvalued. When wise investors are aware that the fundamental prospects of a company have changed so dramatically that its business is declining or the price is excessively high then they will sell and thereby limit their losses. Wise investors exit when the odds are against them.

## Have Reasonable Expectations

A proven path to success in stock investing is to have reasonable expectations. Wise investors expect the stock market to preserve and steadily grow their wealth over time. But investors who view the market as an overnight wealth builder or a slot machine are more likely to chase high growth flavor-of-the-month stocks whose steady growth is far from sustainable. That approach may inevitably lead to the wild pursuit of the most sought after stocks. My own experience shows that the result of chasing performance can be disastrous. Highflying stocks that appreciate at an unreasonably fast pace more often than not plunge at breathtaking speeds.

While stocks have historically proved to be the best vehicle for wealth building, the evidence shows that traditionally this translates to a realistic 9 per cent - 10 per cent annual return. Thus, you should enter the market fully cognizant of this reality and temper your enthusiasm with the reality that any expectation of rapid price appreciation and consistent returns over 10 per cent per annum is generally highly unrealistic.

Even the best fund managers and financial experts often fail to produce returns that are better than the average 10 per cent. You should therefore be satisfied with the fact that you will not beat the market consistently and that in some years you may not achieve expected returns and never rise beyond a maximum 10 per cent return. Even so, you should not take irrational risks on too many speculative or highflying stocks in order to achieve unrealistic double digit returns.

## Reinvest all Dividends

Earning dividends is an excellent way to supplement your income. However, if you are serious about building significant wealth over the long run, your preferred option should be to reinvest dividend income by using it to purchase more stocks. With this approach, dividends increase at a compound rate. You therefore earn dividends on your dividends. This puts your portfolio in a better position to grow exponentially over time than those of your peers. By reinvesting your dividends, over the long term, you will generally outperform those who invest in non-dividend paying stocks.

The most efficient way of reinvesting dividends is to organize automatic dividend reinvestments. Some brokers may allow you to opt to reinvest dividends automatically. This allows you to resist the temptation to spend your dividends. It also allows you to take advantage of periods when the price of the stock is low by automatically purchasing at a discount.

## Diversify (Industry and Size) (Large, Medium and Small Cap Stocks)

*"The only investors who shouldn't diversify are those who are right 100 per cent of the time."*
- Sir John Templeton.

Wise investors never put all their eggs in one basket. For stock investors, this maxim translates into never putting all your savings into one or too few stocks. Diversification also applies not only among individual stocks but also among industries or sectors and among the size of companies you invest in. By selecting a small group of medium and small companies with good businesses and potential for growth along with large well-established companies, you tend to boost the rate of growth of your portfolio. You may also take a few calculated risks by also investing in smaller high growth companies. This primes your portfolio for potential high growth as small and medium companies tend to grow and mature faster than older well established companies.

This approach should however be balanced by investing a large portion of assets in larger, stable companies that have a proven trackrecord of stability and dividend growth. This stabilizes your portfolio when the market has prolonged down periods or when highflying small and medium sized company stocks fall significantly in price.

## Invest Regularly

You would do well to add to your stock holdings on a regular basis. If you have $200,000 to invest in a company, it almost never makes good sense to invest all $200,000 at once. By investing $50,000 and then investing the remaining $150,000 in tranches over time, you could benefit from what is referred to as dollar cost averaging.

With dollar cost averaging, you take advantage of the peaks and troughs of the market. The price of your stock may fall after you invest the first $50,000; so you can purchase the next $150,000 at a lower price. Let's say you buy $50,000 in shares of **GraceKennedy** at $60 per share. On your first purchase, you get 833 shares, if we ignore the fees you pay for the purposes of illustration. If at your next $50,000 purchase the shares have fallen to $50, you now get 1000 shares for the same $50,000. The average cost of your holdings of **GraceKennedy** now becomes less than $55 per share. You spent $100,000 and now have a total of 1833 shares. $100,000 divided by 1833 results in you averaging down the cost you paid for each share from $60 to $54.55.

Only overly confident investors invest large amounts of money at once in a stock because no-one knows where a stock price will go immediately after purchase. Wise investors therefore hedge against this uncertainty by holding some of their funds to invest at regular intervals in order to take advantage of dollar cost averaging. If you are only investing a small amount of money, however, it makes better sense to purchase all the stocks at one time so that you avoid paying multiple trading commissions which would offset any potential gains from dollar cost averaging.

## Buy at a Reasonable Price

*"Whether we're talking about socks or stocks, I like buying quality merchandise when it is marked down."*
- Warren Buffett

This simple principle we apply in our everyday lives, we should apply equally to stock investing. To illustrate the point with a practical example, if gold prices have fallen on the international market, and a gold bracelet that was normally worth $1,200 is on sale for $800, smart shoppers who always wanted to purchase that bracelet would clearly take advantage of this unexpectedly welcome offer. If they buy it for $800, they have a reasonably fair idea that the fall in price will not last forever. As gold prices go up again the same bracelet may, perhaps in two years, be worth $1,500. If buyers then decide to cash in on their good fortune, they would have made a total of $700 on the exquisite bracelet they bought at a marked down price of $800. However, had they bought at the full price of $1,200, they would only have made $300 in profit.

Warren Buffett has argued that in purchasing stocks, a core rule is always to get more for your money than you pay. Valuation is the metric that helps you to determine how much you are getting for what you pay. Valuation indicates how cheap or expensive a stock is. It is a practically immutable law that over time things of value that are cheap will rise in price, and things that are expensive will fall in price. Consequently, wise investors aim to buy a stock when it is cheap so that when everyone suddenly discovers its value and starts buying, the price will rise, making them a good return. Simply put, wise investors are excited to find stocks when they are selling for three quarters or half of what they are worth.

The clear unspoken advantage of buying an undervalued asset is that you get far more than you actually pay for. The same obtains for a company with an undervalued stock price. You pay less for the same good company. This gives you a greater chance of being able to earn enviable profits over the long run as the market discovers the undervalued stock. Wonderful companies become risky investments when people overpay for them.[26]

A good preliminary indication of value is a company's price to earnings (P/E) ratio compared to that of its peers in the same industry. As discussed before, a company's P/E ratio is a measure of the ratio of the company's stock price to its earnings per share. In many ways, a company's P/E ratio is more important than its stock price. This is because the price on its own does not tell you how expensive or how cheap the stock is; the P/E ratio gives the better indication of value. If you understand the ratio you will know that, depending on the P/E ratio, a company whose stock price is $67 is not necessarily more expensive than a company with a price of $27. The P/E ratio indicates the value of a stock, not its price. It is the stock's P/E ratio that tells you whether you are getting a stock at a bargain or are overpaying for it. As we discussed earlier, to arrive at a P/E ratio, you take the price of the share and divide it by the amount per share the company earned in the previous year. This gives an indication of the amount of money the company made on a per share basis.

Let us say the current price of Caribbean Cement is $25 a share. If we divide this price by the company's earnings for the previous 12 months, let's say, $2.50 per share, then $25 divided by $2.50 gives a total of 10. The P/E ratio for Caribbean Cement is therefore 10 in that scenario.

As another example, let us compare the P/E ratios of two companies to see how the P/E ratio can be used to determine whether one company is a better buy than the other. Let us say **Seprod's** share price is $50 and has a P/E ratio of 9 while **GraceKennedy's** share price trades at $25 and has a P/E ratio of 18. In this scenario, **Seprod** is, in reality, cheaper than **GraceKennedy** because it has a lower P/E ratio. The P/E is the number you need to know. In this scenario, **GraceKennedy** trades at 18 times earnings and **Seprod** trades at only 9 times earnings. You are paying 9 times **Seprod's** previous earnings per share for each share you own, but you are paying 18 times **GreaceKennedy's** earnings for each share. That's the real price. It tells us whether we are paying too much or too little for a stock based on its peers in the same industry. Thus, a stock is not a bargain because it trades at, for example, $10; it's a bargain because it trades at 9 times earnings compared to other companies in its industry that trade at 18 times earnings.

A lower P/E ratio therefore tends to indicate that a company is undervalued or that its performance is exceptional compared to its past trends. Although there are limitations to the P/E ratio as a tool for analysis, it is a good rough guide. P/E ratios should normally only be compared for companies in the same industry as comparing P/Es of companies in different industries may not give an accurate picture. As the market discovers undervalued companies, the idea behind the value investing approach is that demand for companies with low P/Es will increase and so will their stock prices. You should bear in mind however that some companies tend to have naturally high P/E ratios because investors are very positive about their future growth prospects.

Investing in stocks based on this approach does not however simply translate into buying low P/E companies. Along with low P/E, you should also look for other factors that demonstrate the underlying value of the company like the future growth prospect of the company; whether it is making profits from its core business; and whether it has sufficient cash to reinvest based on the information recorded in its annual reports.

# Buy and Hold

***"If you aren't willing to own a stock for ten years, don't even think about owning it for ten minutes"***
- Warren Buffett.

Buffett has often said that his favorite period to hold a stock is forever.

The evidence suggests that investors who buy a stock and hold it over the long term despite fluctuations in the market tend to generate greater returns. The term I have come to like most is "buy and snore," the equivalent of Buffett's "buy and hold". Warren Buffett is a devout disciple of this strategy. Buy and hold investors ensure the company they buy is so strong and stable that it will, without doubt, be in business for the next 20 years and even the next 100 years. In that case, it doesn't matter if the market plummets in the next year or oil prices spike or there is a major domestic or global economic crisis. Buy and hold investors buy companies that will survive those developments. Crises and downturns therefore should present no need to sell in a hysterical dash. The important skill is to be disciplined and stick with a good company as long as the fundamentals such as earnings, profits and sales remain good.

Buy and hold does not amount simply to buying any stock and holding for the long run, however. The choice of stock must be informed. Wise investors buy good quality businesses with a strong competitive advantage and run by competent, visionary leadership. When they find such a company, they buy its stock with the intention of holding it for at least 10 to 20 years. Such long hold periods ensure that investors can recover if they enter the market at the wrong time when prices plunge. With shorter periods, you run the risk of leaving a company before it flourishes or selling during a down market at a loss.

Another advantage of the buy and hold strategy is that brokers execute fewer transactions, resulting in reduced brokerage fees. This results in significant savings for the investor over time. The strategy also eliminates the risk of trying to "time the market" or trying to buy when one feels prices are at their lowest as no one can accurately time the market.

## Control Leverage

Wise investors always control leverage. Leverage, in simple terms, refers to borrowing money in order to invest. Brokerage companies and banks may lend a percentage of the purchase value of stocks or other assets in order to encourage investment. This allows investors to purchase more than they would be able to with their own saved funds. Leverage can be useful for the sophisticated investor who has sound knowledge of the risks involved. Leverage is not however for every investor and is certainly not a strategy I recommend for the individual investor with little experience. Levered funds invested poorly can leave the investor with vast levels of uncontrollable debt.

Wise investors ensure that they are knowledgeable about the investment for which they use leverage. Secondly, they only borrow amounts that they can repay easily even if their investment fails.

# Be Patient

*"Successful investing takes time, discipline and patience. No matter how great the talent or effort, some things just take time: You can't produce a baby in one month by getting nine women pregnant."*
— Warren Buffett.

Patience is a crucial strategy for winning in the stock market. Yet, it is probably the hardest to adhere to. Former U.S. President Ronald Reagan said it succinctly: *"Don't just do something, stand there."* This is the best antidote to investors who feel they must do something with their portfolios by trading aggressively at regular intervals. The evidence shows that this lack of patience tends to be costly. It is costly because investors lose upside gains when the company rebounds as well as by paying regular brokerage fees. Investors may also lose by selling an appreciating stock too quickly. They may decide that the stock has appreciated 100 per cent so they should take their profits, only to realize that having sold an excellent company, the stock price again doubles and then doubles a third time. The investor who overtrades typically chronically underperforms the market.

Peter Kundhart, the Emmy Award winning producer of the 2017 documentary *"Becoming Warren Buffett,"* had the benefit of spending considerable amounts of time with the investor and confirmed that the biggest takeaway from the legendary investor's life is learning to be patient. For Kundhart, all investors have the capacity to exercise the patience that generates substantial returns.

In summarizing Buffett's approach to investing, Kundhart said of

Buffett, *"he feels that once you connect with a company that you like- a company that you believe in- you should stick it out for the long haul... And that's what he's done. He buys stocks for life. Unless something dramatic happens that changes his mind, he can live through the ups and downs because he knows that at the centre of it is a healthy company that he believes in.[27]"*

## Ignore the Stock Price

This may sound a bit alarming, but it has significant value. The daily or weekly movement of stock prices tends to be a significant distraction. What stock prices do today or tomorrow or next month is not very important over the long term. Investors who focus on the daily or weekly gyrations of a stock price and react to or worry about those moves will likely be unsuccessful. The price of a stock often does not reflect the true value of a company; it is just a guidepost that can change at any moment. The market is often wrong about the price of a company. Many good companies fall in price while some companies that may have poor prospects rise in price. Price movements are therefore a bad indicator to follow. You should not be overly preoccupied with price movements as these are often inaccurate reflections of a stock's true prospect. You should not necessarily therefore sell stocks of a good company that falls in price as over time the market will value the company as it should.

## Ignore the Market

*"People who succeed in the stock market also accept periodic losses, setbacks, and unexpected occurrences. Calamitous drops*

*do not scare them out of the game"*[28]

Wise investors are not overly preoccupied with general market swings. The stock market will swing up and down on a regular basis. The investors who ultimately perform well are those who ignore these temporary gyrations. It is counterproductive to sell when markets are down and buy when markets are up. Yet this is what many investors do and thereby limit the potential for portfolio growth over time. No-one can predict where a market will go in a month or six months or even a year. However, the only sure prediction that has stood the test of time is that over the long term, that is 5 or 10 years, markets tend to move up. Patient investors who ignore downward swings are therefore likely to be successful. That is because they are investing in good companies not the stock market.

## Ignore Tips

Wise investors ignore stock tips. Tips are for waiters, as they say. More often than not people think they know what will happen next with a stock. In reality, they do not know unless they are insiders at the company in which case they are prohibited from giving tips. Tips are often worthless information that if acted on could result in serious losses to the investor.

## Look for Companies with Good Finances

You should select companies that are in good financial shape. This means that these companies' debt levels should be low and their revenues, profits and earnings should be increasing. Before investing in a company, it is worthwhile to take a look at its balance sheet if possible. Too much debt on a company's balance sheet may signal potential problems in the future. However, some fast growing companies with excellent potential may need to take on debt in order to grow. In some cases, therefore, a company's debt should not necessarily be a huge disadvantage if it is justified based on its future growth prospect.

## Don't Overinvest

You can't be an expert on everything. You can't research every stock sufficiently well to be able to buy them with conviction. It therefore makes little sense to try to purchase too many companies and expect to profit. This amounts to over diversification. While diversification is important, you should manage it properly. You should only buy as many companies as you can manageably research and keep abreast of. There is no point in holding 20 or 30 companies in your portfolio unless you are fortunate enough to have a full day each day to devote to studying them. A minimum of five and a maximum of 15 stocks is perhaps ideal for an individual investor. In stock investing, less can mean more. That is, the fewer well managed companies that you understand and invest in the more likely you will hit a home run on the very best stocks. Learn a few stocks well and profit from them.

## Don't Be Fooled by Past Performance

The past performance of a company is no guarantee of where its stock price will be in the future. An obsessive focus on how a stock has performed in the past as an indicator of where it will go in the future is an extremely dangerous approach for stock investors. Many companies have performed spectacularly over a period of years or months only to fall precipitously. Similarly, many companies have remained stagnant for long periods before the market recognized their potential, resulting in meteoric rises in their stock prices. If anything, stock investors must focus on the future of the company as their primary concern.

## Favour Limit Orders

Always use limit orders when buying or selling stocks. Market orders leave the investor at the whim of the market. Once you decide what price you wish to buy or sell a stock at, request that price. By using a limit order, you buy or sell at the price you want. Otherwise, you may find yourself overpaying for or underselling a stock.

## Control Your Emotions

The more anxious you get about market movements, and the more you allow yourself to act based on fear or excitement, the more likely you are to make costly errors. So when a stock or the market is moving higher and higher, never think that you must get in on the action. Similarly, when the market or a stock is falling, fear should never be the determining factor in the decisions you make. Without fail, emotional reactions to a stock or the market lead to underperformance. Discipline is the most important quality in winning as an investor. Sometimes discipline requires that you admit that you missed an opportunity and that it's too late to act.

## Keep doing Your Homework

Successful investors' homework does not end when they purchase a stock. They must keep abreast of the company's story. On a monthly or quarterly basis, you should keep reading about the company's performance at least half an hour per week per stock so that you are in a good position to know whether the company's story has changed for the worse. Good sources of information are the company's annual and quarterly reports, broker analyses, annual general meetings, and important newspaper articles.

Complacent investors, who refuse to keep abreast of a company's development, run the risk of a good investment becoming a disastrous one. Money cannot manage itself, so the investor must manage and monitor his investments consistently. You should, at least every six months, assess your investments to make sure your assumptions about the growth of the business still hold true. The main piece of information in your research should be to discover whether the company is growing faster than its peers. You should focus on facts and empirical data about the company or business and monitor trends and new developments in the company's industry. Where the market has completely changed or where the business no longer has a good prospect of success, you should adjust your asset allocation to more productive uses. Building wealth requires investors to allocate much of their time and energy to this exercise.

# Notes

[20] https://wallethub.com/edu/market-share-by-credit-card-network/25531/

[21] http://www.cnbc.com/2016/12/23/amazon-grabbing-the-bulk-of-surging-online-sales-this-holiday.html

[22] Peter Lynch- One Up on Wall Street: How to Use What You Know to Make Money on Wall Street" page 109.

[23] Peter Lynch- One Up on Wall Street: How to Use What You Know to Make Money on Wall Street" page 13

[24] http://www.simplysafedividends.com/dividend-kings-list/

[25] http://www.simplysafedividends.com/dividend-kings-list/

[26] Peter Lynch- One Up on Wall Street: How to Use What You Know to Make Money on Wall Street" page 14

[27] http://www.cnbc.com/2017/02/20/producer-of-becoming-warren-buffett-shares-his-biggest-takeaway-from-working-with-the-billionaire.html

[28] Peter Lynch- One Up on Wall Street: How to Use What You Know to Make Money on Wall Street" page 75.

# GENERAL PRINCIPLES TO CONSIDER BEFORE INVESTING IN STOCKS

The System for Building Wealth

Amateur Investors Can Win in Stocks

Stock Investment is not Gambling

Change Your Mindset

Think Big

Fear Inhibits Success

Accept That Failure is the Beginning, not the End

Take Action

Set Financial Goals

# GENERAL PRINCIPLES TO CONSIDER BEFORE INVESTING IN STOCKS

The ultimate reason investors buy stocks is to build wealth. There are certain basic principles which, if they bear in mind, may help them to become better investors. You should understand these general principles even before beginning the journey of investing in stocks.

## The System for Building Wealth

There is a system for building wealth. A tiny one per cent of the world population owns over fifty per cent of the world's wealth. These individuals hit upon the formula of spectacular wealth creation. They have discovered potent secrets that appear to be off-limits to the rest of the world. What could they be? One of the primary strategies in the system for building wealth is investment in the stock market. I will therefore set out some general principles below which you should bear in mind before investing in stocks.

## Amateur Investors Can Win in Stocks

Many individuals discover early that even as amateur stock investors they can succeed. In his book *"Beating the Street,"* Peter Lynch showed that amateur investors who devote even a small amount of time studying companies in an industry they have some knowledge about can outperform 95 per cent of paid financial experts who manage mutual funds[29]. He cited the case of a group of seventh grade students at St. Agnes School in Arlington Massachusetts who in 1990 produced a two-year investment return of 70 per cent that was spectacularly higher than the returns of Wall Street professionals. In the same period, the S&P 500 composite index, a general US stock benchmark that professional investors try to beat, gained a modest 26 per cent by contrast[30]. The St. Agnes amateurs outperformed 99 per cent of all equity mutual funds whose managers were paid handsomely for their expertise in fund management. Mr Lynch also persuasively tells the story of a group of amateur investors in investment clubs who consistently beat the average returns of the so-called Wall Street experts[31]. These examples show that you do not need to be a professional investor to succeed in stock market investing.

## Stock Investment is not Gambling

Distinguishing stock investing from gambling is critical. One of the misconceptions about stock investing is that it is tantamount to gambling. Nothing could be farther from the truth. Unlike gamblers, investors don't lose in the end provided they follow the rules that put the odds in their favour. The odds are always against the gambler because there is no proven method or formula to win. Gambling is purely a game of chance. The odds in the lottery or at the racetrack are always set against the player. Investing, on the other hand, involves a deliberate, systematic approach that guarantees a return in the long run.

# Change Your Mindset

*"The starting point of all achievement is DESIRE. Keep this constantly in mind. Weak desire brings weak results, just as a small fire makes a small amount of heat."*
- Napoleon Hill: "Think and Grow Rich"

It is the way the rich think that truly makes them rich. Their philosophy that making money is a right rather than a privilege and their intense desire to build wealth propels them to vast fortunes. It is also by thinking like the wealthy that average investors will be able first to accumulate enough savings to invest in stocks.

One of my favourite books on the subject of the mind-set of the rich is *"How the Rich Think,"* a classic volume by Steve Siebold. For Mr Siebold, *"world-class thinkers know in a capitalist country they have the right to be rich if they're willing to create massive value for others."*[32]

Those who become wealthy view wealth as a right and not a privilege. Without exception, all wealthy persons had to change their outlook on money before they became wealthy. They first developed an intense, unshakeable and unbending desire to become wealthy then cultivated a mind-set that conceived of wealth as an entitlement. In the same way, prospective stock investors must develop the mind-set that allows them over time to accumulate enough savings for investments in stocks.

In contrast to the wealthy, the poor tend to cultivate a completely opposite mind-set. They take the view that they are not entitled, nor have the right, nor the skills nor the resources to be rich. The poor tell themselves that they do not have the ability nor skill to build wealth.

On the other hand, self-made wealth builders persuade themselves that they are as good as the wealthiest one per cent in the world and that they deserve to be financially independent. They tell themselves that wealth is not off limits. It is that mind-set that propels them to develop a system to generate wealth. In other words, they believe that if others can gain wealth through stock investing, they can do the same thing by learning and applying the same formula that successful investors have applied.

Cameron Smith, for instance, in his book *"The Top Ten Distinctions between Millionaires and the Middle Class"* confirms that the US millionaires' way of thinking is the key factor that distinguishes them from those who fail to achieve financial independence. He has argued that those who eventually become wealthy tend to ask themselves empowering questions. In contrast, the poor and middle class ask disempowering ones. The empowering questions people who become rich ask themselves focus on what they can do to acquire the wealth they aspire to earn. The middle class ask less far-reaching questions which focus on their current circumstances rather than on a formula for wealth creation. Smith suggests that the questions one asks determine the results one gets. Therefore, the very first step even for stock investors is to develop a mind-set that sees financial independence as a right and not a privilege. The second step is to think about how to use proven stock investment principles to achieve financial independence.

# Think Big
*"For as [a man] thinketh in his heart so is he.*[33]*"*

Many persons fail to reach big financial goals because they fail to push beyond what they expect. They often fail to think beyond savings and consider wider options such as stock investing. The wealth builders who succeed free themselves of self-imposed limitations and move outside of their comfort zone to hit a target farther than they had originally contemplated. In the business of achieving financial independence, this often means a willingness to consider one of the greatest sources of wealth building, namely stock investing.

Thinking big is a central commandment of those who succeed in the stock market; but the greatest obstacle to big thinking is fear.

## Fear Inhibits Success

Fear is the enemy of big thinking and often the one emotion that turns people off from investing in stocks. Investors often hear stories about stock market crashes and stock price falls and then get scared of investing in stocks. Fear can rob anyone, including investors, out of great financial or other achievements in their lifetime. Readers need only look at examples around them to see that great success in any sphere of life is a function of overcoming fear. Usain Bolt, the fastest man in the world, became a success by overcoming paralyzing fear. Bolt relates his journey to success by recounting one of his first international athletic meets, the 2002 World Junior Championships in Kingston. As a 15 year old, competing for the first time at the national level in a crowd of thousands, he became crippled by fear.

His mother, in an interview, said very pointedly that, *"he didn't want to go...he was afraid to go up against the other boys who were bigger and more powerful than him. He was afraid to lose."*[34]

With gentle coaxing, Bolt overcame that fear and participated in the Games winning gold and two silver medals. After becoming the most successful track athlete in Olympics history, Bolt disclosed that, *"The world juniors made me who I am today."*[35] By the 2016 Olympics in Brazil, Bolt had become an eight time Olympic gold medallist. He accomplished the hitherto impossible feat of winning the 100m and 200m sprint in three consecutive Olympic Games. He became an 11- time world champion, winning consecutive world championship 100m, 200m and 4x100m relay gold medals from 2009 to 2015. He broke the 200m world record twice setting 19.30 in 2008 and 19.19 in 2009. In recognition of his extraordinary feats, he was named IAAF World Athlete of the Year, Track and Field Athlete of the Year and Laureus World Sportsman of the Year four times. If Usain Bolt had not overcome his fear, he would certainly never have become a global Olympic legend.

The same principle applies to the big thinking mentality required of the stock investors. Most successful stock investors will confirm that overcoming the fear of investing in stocks has been one of the key sources of wealth creation in their own lives.

## Accept That Failure is the Beginning, not the End

Sir James Dyson, a British inventor, became renowned for his innovative bagless, transparent Dyson vacuum cleaner. Dyson's vacuum cleaner became the best-selling vacuum cleaner by revenue in the United States. In one of his interviews, Sir Dyson admitted that he made 5,127 prototypes of his vacuum before he got it right. He admits he failed 5,126 times. He makes the important point however that he learned from each failure.

The profile of Peter Munk[36], the founder of Barrick Gold - a colossus in the mining world is also a compelling example of how prospective investors should view failures. Mr Munk's profile records some of the most insightful lessons on the importance of converting threats into opportunities and transforming failures into lifelong successes. In the piece, the author commented on a catalogue of failures faced by Mr Munk and his record of transforming them into the most unbelievable successes. Mr Munk, a former refugee from the Nazis, escaped his native Hungary in 1944 with hundreds of Jews who managed to avoid the gas chambers by entering Switzerland. On his arrival in Canada in 1948, his family fortune was completely dissipated but with steely determination, he managed to study for a degree in electronic engineering by working his way through college. He engaged in a variety of odd jobs such as selling Christmas trees and cleaning cars. His initial business venture that he named the Clairtone Sound Corporation flourished, only to collapse spectacularly in 11 years as a result of competition from Japanese rivals and an unwise expansion campaign.

The poverty-stricken immigrant had risen to the zenith of corporate success only to plunge to the depths of failure with his life's investment in Clairtone Sound turning to ashes under his feet. This failure, however, bore in it a valuable lesson that framed his business philosophy and marked the foundation of the extraordinary success of Barrick Gold.

Having learnt from Clairtone Sound that every human being makes mistakes, he wisely concluded that he had to hedge so that if he made a mistake in a business venture he would still have the ability to continue in the game. It was a brilliant strategy that he employed to great effect in Barrick Gold. While his competitors in other mining outfits were gambling heavily in the business and losing, he hedged, resulting in his company soaring.

Mr Munk faced many other failures before the success of Barrick Gold. For example, he invested heavily in the hotel sector in the South Pacific and Egypt - ventures that again failed. He also invested in the development of a business park in Berlin that failed to match competing parks in the city. The failure of Clairtone Sound and other business ventures did not deter his willingness to undertake new businesses. Mr Munk was not daunted. He could easily have thrown in the towel, but he resolved to dust himself off and continue in the game, hence his ultimate success with Barrick Gold.

Mr. Munk's experience shows the prospective investor that a key ingredient in overcoming failure is the willingness to forge ahead even when some of your investments do not work out. Failures will be inevitable. Even the best stock investors make mistakes. The mark of ultimate success, however, is the willingness to learn from those mistakes and forge ahead.

## Take Action

Not everyone who agrees that stocks are a good source of wealth creation will invest in stocks. People often meet only ten to twenty per cent of their goals because a decision without action is as bad as no decision at all.

Taking action to invest in stocks as a source of wealth creation is an indispensable ingredient of success for the prospective wealth builder. Edward Rickenbacker (1842 - 1914) put it in very blunt terms by saying, *"There's a six-word formula for success: Think things through, then follow through."* Would-be wealth builders must therefore first think big, then translate their vision into concrete daily steps by first writing and following a strategy for stock investing.

This strategy could start with the essentials of stock market investing discussed above which resonate most with you.

You must however start immediately, not in another ten minutes, or another hour, or worse yet tomorrow or next week. You should not feed procrastination. You should tell yourself every day that it must be done NOW, not a minute later. Starting the journey immediately may mean the very difference between success and failure.

## Set Financial Goals

In order to maximize success, as a stock investor, you should write a clear statement of your financial goals. This is non-negotiable. It is also imperative that you review your goals from time to time, making slight adjustments as necessary.

You should break down your overall goal into intermediate and short-term time bound goals. They may be weekly, monthly or yearly goals. So while your overall goal may be to accumulate $50,000,000 by age 55, your immediate goal may be to save 5 per cent of your gross income in the first year to invest. Short term and intermediate goals are usually measurable and realistic. If they are not realistic, these goals will lead to frustration and you may be tempted to abandon them. You should therefore start modestly but become increasingly ambitious as time progresses. Your initial 5 per cent saving may increase in the second year to perhaps 7 per cent and then 10 per cent of your gross income in the third year. The ultimate mid-term goal may be to save a maximum of 20 per cent of your pre-tax income from which to invest.

There is no substitute for a written financial plan. With a written financial plan, as a prospective stock investor you are compelled to move from words to action.

# Notes

[29] Peter Lynch, Beating the Street p 19.

[30] Peter Lynch, Beating the Street p 26.

[31] Peter Lynch, Beating the Street p 32-33.

[32] Steve Siebold

[33] Proverbs 23:7

[34] Anna Kessel, "Usain Bolt still loves to party and still hates to train", The Guardian, April 11, 2009, accessed May 28, 2014, **http://www.theguardian.com/sport/2009/apr/11/usain-bolt-athletics-interview-records-100m.**

[35] Anna Kessel, "Usain Bolt still loves to party and still hates to train", The Guardian, April 11, 2009, accessed May 28, 2014, **http://www.theguardian.com/sport/2009/apr/11/usain-bolt-athletics-interview-records-100m.**

[36] Munk's Tale, How a former refugee from the Nazis made and lost several fortunes, Economist.com/blogs/Schumpeter, April 19, 2014.

# SAVING TO INVEST IN STOCKS

Fill Your Basket

Automate Your Savings

Increase Your Earnings Over Time

Put the Pruning Knife to Good Effect

Eliminate High Interest Debt

Avoid Lifestyle Inflation

Build Multiple Sources of Income

Apply the Latte Factor

Keep an Emergency Fund

# SAVING TO INVEST IN STOCKS

In this Chapter, I will address a few practical steps on how an investor can save consistently to invest in stocks. Since wealth creation strategies are universal across asset classes, the principles below will often reaffirm what we have so far discussed with some nuances.

## Fill Your Basket

Many of us would have heard the saying: *"one one cocoa full basket,"* meaning that a basket of ground provisions is filled eventually by adding single items to it over time. Ten per cent or more of your income saved consistently is one of the basic starting points. An empty basket, signifying no savings is a recipe for financial failure. By consistently saving at least 10 per cent of your income specifically for investment purposes your ability to invest in stocks will significantly increase.

## Automate Your Savings

You won't spend what you don't see. You may therefore want to set up an automatic transfer at the bank from a salary account to a savings/investment account. Automatic transfers represent one of the best time tested strategies to save for investment. It is convenient and you will not run the risk of forgetting to make the transfer. As time progresses you will discover that your savings grow enough to begin making worthwhile investments.

## Increase Your Earnings Over Time

Unless you are born into wealth, own a business, win the lottery or inherit a fortune, you need to work with others to earn an income to invest. Whether you earn a weekly wage or monthly salary or a stipend, one of the most useful routes to accumulating enough to invest is to find ways to increase your income over time. Prospective investors who earn a salary and wish to invest must therefore find ways to set themselves apart from their peers and become more valuable to their employers.

The more valuable you are, the more likely your salary will increase over time affording you additional income to invest. You may increase your value in many ways. Having a growth mind-set, as explained by Carol Dweck in her book *"Mindset: The New Psychology of Success,"* is a basic requirement. People with a growth mind-set are oriented towards learning. Further study in their field to upgrade skills and knowledge and sharpen their expertise is the classic example. There is also no substitute for distinguishing oneself through hard work. Prospective investors who distinguish themselves and increase their value should not be afraid to ask for a salary increase when they genuinely bring more value to their organization than they are compensated for. Few bosses will ignore a pitch that demonstrates an employee's value and how their companies or organizations will benefit.

## Put the Pruning Knife to Good Effect

Prospective investors should track everything they spend and find ways to eliminate expenses or reduce them. *"The man is richest whose pleasures are the cheapest.*[37]*"*

My advice is that you track exactly where your income goes every month and find luxuries that can be cut. The more you reduce your expenses, the more likely you will save enough to invest in the market. The value of frugality is aptly demonstrated in the United States, where one of the ancestry groups with the highest concentrations of millionaire households are Scottish Americans. One reason is that Scottish-Americans are notorious for being more frugal than persons of other ancestries. Thomas Stanley and William Donka in their book *"The Millionaire Next Door"* notoriously described them as living in self-designed environments of relative scarcity.

Vicki Robin and Joe Dominguez's approach to cutting expenses is also worth adopting. The authors of *Your Money or Your Life* explain that any money you earn costs you time. Therefore, a Tastee Patty worker who earns the equivalent of US$10 an hour exchanges one whole hour of her life to acquire those US$10. If she works eight hours per day she earns the equivalent of US$80. According to Vicki Robin's approach, that same worker, like all prospective investors, should think of everything she wants to purchase in terms of the number of hours of her life that she would have to give up to get that item.

So the Tastee Patty worker who is about to spend the equivalent of US$100 for a ticket to a party at Frenchman's Cove should consider the purchase as costing her more than a whole day of her working life. The question she should ask is whether it is truly worth exchanging more than an entire day of her life to attend the party. The same applies to any purchase. You should calculate how much of your life it costs you and decide whether it is worth it. This type of analysis quickly puts impulse buys into perspective and tends to be a very good strategy to cut back on impulsive spending.

In other words, the prospective investor *"never eats his seed corn."* Wise farmers know that every seed of corn they have can either be eaten or has the potential to be planted for another harvest.

Those farmers who eat their seeds and fail to replant run the risk of destroying their own livelihoods. In the same way, every dollar you spend could have been used to generate hundreds of dollars over a period of years from interests, profits, dividends and capital appreciation. If one dollar could have generated $400 over time, you could see every such dollar as costing one dollar plus $400. So with every dollar you spend, ask yourself, *"What is the future value of this dollar?"* Then decide if you are willing to pay that cost. In other words, apply the "pruning knife" to cut your expenses in order to afford yourself more seed corn for a more bountiful harvest.

# Eliminate High Interest Debt

*"The rich rule over the poor, and the borrower is a servant to the lender."*[38]

The wise investor should only assume good debt. Good debt, as famously described by financial advisor Robert Kyosaki, is debt used to purchase assets that produce a return. The investor who wants to invest in the stock market should aim to assume good debt if he has to assume any debt at all. Having assumed debt, you should prioritize the repayment of those debts in order of interest rates. The better approach is to pay off those debts with the highest interest rates while continuing to pay at least the minimum on all other debts. By using that strategy, your total debt payment over the long run will be less, leaving more money for investment.

# Avoid Lifestyle Inflation

You become a victim of lifestyle inflation when you increase your spending as your income increases. If you could make do with a Suzuki Swift, you now believe that with your promotion to manager, you should buy a Lexus in keeping with your new status. As another example, law school graduates who become practising lawyers may also think that with a higher salary they should now purchase a 5 bedroom house or a more expensive luxury car as befits their new status. This is often referred to as the golden handcuff. As income increases, workers voluntarily submit themselves to the trap of increased spending to demonstrate to the world that they are successful.

There is nothing quite as dangerous for would-be investors as the temptation to outwardly show the trappings of academic or professional success through conspicuous consumption. Lifestyle inflation is self-defeating for would-be investors. It competes for savings and investment resources. At its most costly, it destroys or delays by several decades investors' goal of financial freedom. If you wish to find ways to ensure significant savings for investment in stocks, my recommendation would be to avoid the trap of lifestyle inflation by saving every salary increase, investing it in its entirety; or at the very least, a significant percentage of it. Every windfall, whether it is a salary increase or bonus, should be seen as an investment seed and opportunity to further leapfrog towards your goal of financial independence.

## Build Multiple Sources of Income

Anyone who aims to invest should identify various sources from which to earn an income from which to invest. The average person who achieves significant financial success has various sources of income. Relying exclusively on a single source of income is never sufficient to save enough for investment.

Everyone is blessed with 24 hours a day, but only has on average 8 hours to devote to work. Employees who work for others and earn a salary or active income will almost never get ahead. But individuals who have other sources of income such as businesses which generate cash are better able to invest. They earn passive income that supplements their active income.

As an example, you could put in place a system to earn from the following sources of income simultaneously:

1.   A salary;
2.   Income from a business you own;
3.   Rental income;
4.   Royalties or patents from works you have created, for example, a book you have written; and
5.   Interest on savings.

## Apply the Latte Factor

In his book *"The Automatic Millionaire,"* David Bach discussed what he called the latte factor. In essence, it is as follows: consider your casual day-to-day spending habits. A latte at Starbucks could go from between the equivalent of US$1.50 to $3.50. Many people tend to pick up a latte or coffee on the way to work in the mornings without a second thought. In the Jamaican context, it may be lunch at a nearby restaurant. It seems like a cheap indulgence that only costs the equivalent of US$1.50 or US$3.50. But had that money been saved and placed in a simple interest bearing account over a long period, the results would be astounding. Individuals who successfully accumulate money to invest in stocks know this so they start by eliminating the metaphorical lattes from their daily lives.

The equivalent of US$1.50 not spent on a morning coffee on your way to work saves you US$7.50 per week in a five-day work week. Over a period of one year, you could save the equivalent of US$360 by continuing to resist the indulgence day after day, and simply placing that saving every month in an account that yields 6 per cent per annum compounded. After 20 years, this could amount to a total of over US$ 14, 000. If you manage to keep doing this for thirty years, the result of over US$30,000 is even better.

Resisting the simple indulgence of a US$3.50 latte five days a week would yield, with a 6 per cent compound interest, over $30,000 over 20 years and over US$70,000 over 30 years. That's just the saving from one cup of coffee. Consider the possibilities if you save on other small indulgences over time and invest. Even an investment in a boring 2 per cent savings account with little risk over time could yield great rewards.

Let's consider how you would fare if you applied this principle to more than coffee. Let's say you decided to take lunch to work rather than pay the equivalent of US$10 per day at the nearby deli. You would then save an extra US$2,400 per year. That is US$50 per week over five days and US$ 2,400 per year.

Over 20 years, this amount, compounded at 6 per cent, would result in you accumulating over US$93,500. Over 30 years, you would be over US$200,000 richer. That would certainly end up shaving a few years off your working life allowing you to retire earlier.

Let's add a third indulgence that can easily be eliminated. Let's say you decide to give up the extra cable package with those additional 40 channels you never watch. You decide to go with a more modest cable channel package with the channels you actually watch. You have now cut your cable bill from the equivalent of US$100 per month to

US$50. That simple $50 per month could lead to significant savings over just ten years.

One well used formula to calculate a weekly expense compounded over ten years is to multiply the price by 752. To calculate a monthly expense compounded over ten years multiply the price by 173. Using our formula, our US$50 per month savings from cable alone would give us more than an extra US$8,600 in only ten years.

So the next time you think of what may seem to be a simple expense, use the formula above and ask yourself if it's worth it. You should therefore think of all of your purchases as having long-term consequences, not as a short-term event. So the more you intend to save in order to invest in stocks, think of an expense not in terms of this week or this month but in terms of how much it would be worth accumulated over 10 to 20 years.

## Keep an Emergency Fund

At any moment an unexpected event may occur for which you will need readily available cash. Without warning, you may become unemployed, a sudden illness may occur, your car may require major repairs or something catastrophic may happen.

With an emergency fund, you need not be anxious about dipping into your savings reserved for investment. In order to avoid having to suddenly sell stocks, possibly at a down period in the market, or withdraw money from your retirement account, you should have cash readily available. Setting up an emergency cash fund with at least

5 months' worth of living expenses is a good rule of thumb. Allow that money to sit in a safe place where it is accessible immediately. With an emergency fund on hand, you can allow your investments to grow untouched even when unexpected emergencies arise.

What are the practical steps to building an emergency fund? Some people dislike the thought of building up 5 to 6 months of living expenses. The first step, however, is to start by setting a manageable, small target. This could be an overall target of $60,000 further reduced to more achievable targets by setting a goal of perhaps $5,000 a week. This would allow you to achieve your $60,000 target in 3 months. By reaching your $60,000 goal in a few months or less, you will feel a sense of accomplishment. You then have an incentive to set and achieve higher targets over time.

# Notes

[37] Henry David Thoreau.
[38] Proverbs 22:7.

# THE ULTIMATE WEALTH - THE WISDOM OF THE CONEY

# THE ULTIMATE WEALTH – THE WISDOM OF THE CONEY

*"The conies are but a feeble folk, yet make they their houses in the rocks."*[39]

The Proverbs mention the conies as being among the four wisest creatures on earth. What distinguishes the coney and illustrates its great wisdom is the fact that it makes its house in the rocks.

To understand the true wisdom of the coney, one must understand the metaphorical meaning of the Rock, and there are plenty of clues in biblical texts to point us to it. One of these clues is the parable of the wise and the foolish builder. The wise man digs deep and lays the foundation of his house on a rock, while the foolish man builds his house on sand[40]. When the storms rage, the house on the rock remains, but the house built on sand crumbles.

Coney (hyrax siriacus), translated from the Hebrew word "shaphan," means "the hider." Conies once inhabited the Arabian Peninsula and Israel. Their size and colour are similar to a rabbit, but they have no tail. Because their feet are not designed for digging, they always make their homes in the clefts of rocks. Part of the explanation for this may be that the coney is inherently vulnerable. It has weak teeth, short incisors and is practically defenceless--so it wisely finds comfort in the rock.

Humans also need a force greater than they are. There are things of far greater import than money, and wise investors would do well to take note. Investment accounts become useless when faced with life changing events. Steve Jobs, the late founder, chairman and CEO of Apple, was among the wealthiest men in America. He had a net worth of approximately US$7 billion. At the peak of his career, some described him as nothing short of legendary. Yet when Jobs was diagnosed with cancer in 2003, despite the best medical services the world could provide, Jobs died at a relatively young age in October, 2011.

Man's vulnerability mirrors the vulnerability of the coney; and the man who truly values life will find the path that reflects the wisdom of the coney: ***"We are best served by finding and making our home in the Rock-the source of life and by acknowledging God as the source of all blessings."***

Prospective investors would be wise to remember that true wealth only comes from the blessing of God for *"the blessing of the Lord, it maketh rich, and he addeth no sorrow with it.[41]"* This is the first limb of the wisdom of the coney.

The second limb of the wisdom of the coney is that ultimately, the real objective of wealth is to make our societies better and improve the lives of fellow human beings. It may be this lesson that some of the wealthiest have already learned. Some of the best-known US billionaires and millionaires have pledged to give away their fortunes before they die. We could in fact go back to the early 1900s for good examples.

Andrew Carnegie, the famous Scottish American businessman who helped pioneer America's steel industry, became one of the richest men in history. In the last 18 years before he died, he gave away millions (approximately US$76 billion in 2015 value) amounting to some 90 per cent of his wealth to charities, universities and foundations. In his 1889 article, *"The Gospel of Wealth,"* he urged the rich to use their wealth to improve society. He wrote, *"...the amassing of wealth is one of the worse species of idolatry. No idol more debasing than the worship of money[42]."*

In keeping with his later focus on philanthropy, Mr. Carnegie also argued that, *"... The man who dies thus rich dies disgraced.[43]"* The lesson, in his words, is that those who manage to accumulate wealth should never die with accumulated wealth. Their duty is first to ensure the basic needs of their dependants and then to distribute the remaining wealth to the benefit of society. Michael Bloomberg with a net worth at June 2016 of over US$45 billion,[44] took the same approach. He famously said, *"I am a big believer in giving it all away and have always said that the best financial planning ends with bouncing the cheque to the undertaker."* [45] Following Andrew Carnegie's example, many of the world's wealthiest have committed to give most of their wealth to philanthropy. Bill and Melinda Gates formed the Bill and Melinda Gates Foundation as a platform from which to support charity. It is one of the largest private foundations in the world and aims to reduce poverty and improve healthcare worldwide.

Through the Foundation, Bill and Melinda Gates, who rank among the richest persons in the world, have devoted a large portion of their wealth to charity. Warren Buffett, the second richest man in the world in 2015, pledged a significant amount of his wealth to the Foundation through shares in his company Berkshire Hathaway. In a story reporting that he had given his kids' charities $600 million, Buffett committed to giving all of his shares in Berkshire Hathaway, worth billions of dollars, to charity[46]. Similarly, the billionaire Mark Zuckerberg, the founder of Facebook and his wife, Priscilla Chan, committed to give most of their wealth away over time.

The Giving Pledge is also a symbol of the true purpose for wealth creation. It is a commitment by the wold's wealthiest individuals and families to give most of their wealth away.

Many millionaires continue to use the Giving Pledge as their tool for charity. A profile of contributors to the Giving Pledge is at www.givingpledge.org. The site reflects a who's who among the world's wealthy. The commitment letters on the site give useful insights into the motivations of the wealthy for giving away vast amounts of their wealth. In all cases, they came to the conclusion, after amassing vast amounts of wealth, that helping and caring for others is far more important than money.

Unless accumulated wealth is used in the service of mankind, the acquisition of wealth is an empty pursuit. Prospective investors must also focus their undivided attention on building a life of quality focused on family, friends and faith. Take out one of those components from the equation, and the investor's life will be the poorer for it.

*"For what shall it profit a man if he shall gain the whole world and lose his own soul[47]?"*

# Notes

[39] Proverbs 30: 26

[40] St Luke 5: 48-49.

[41] Proverbs 10:22

[42] Klein, Muray (2004) The Change Makers, p.57, Macmillan

[43] Burlingame, Dwigth (2004) Philanthropy in America p.60

[44] The Richest; Richest Businessmen, Richest politicians at **http://www.therichest.com/ celebnetworth/politician/michael-bloomberg-net-worth/ retrieved March 23, 2017.**

[45] Mike Backs Warren Buffett and Bill Gates Call to Donate more to Charity by Businessweek June 17, 2010 at **https://www.mikebloomberg.com/news/mike-backs-warren-buffett-bill-gates-call-to-donate-more-to-charity/ retrieved March 23, 2017.**

[46] Warren, Buffett, on his birthday, gives kids 600 million by Josh Funk of Associated Press at **http://www.nbcnews.com/business/warren-buffett-his-birthday-gives-kids-600m-972645 Retrieved March 23, 2017.**

[47] Mark 8:36

www.ingramcontent.com/pod-product-compliance
Lightning Source LLC
Chambersburg PA
CBHW032006190326
41520CB00007B/373